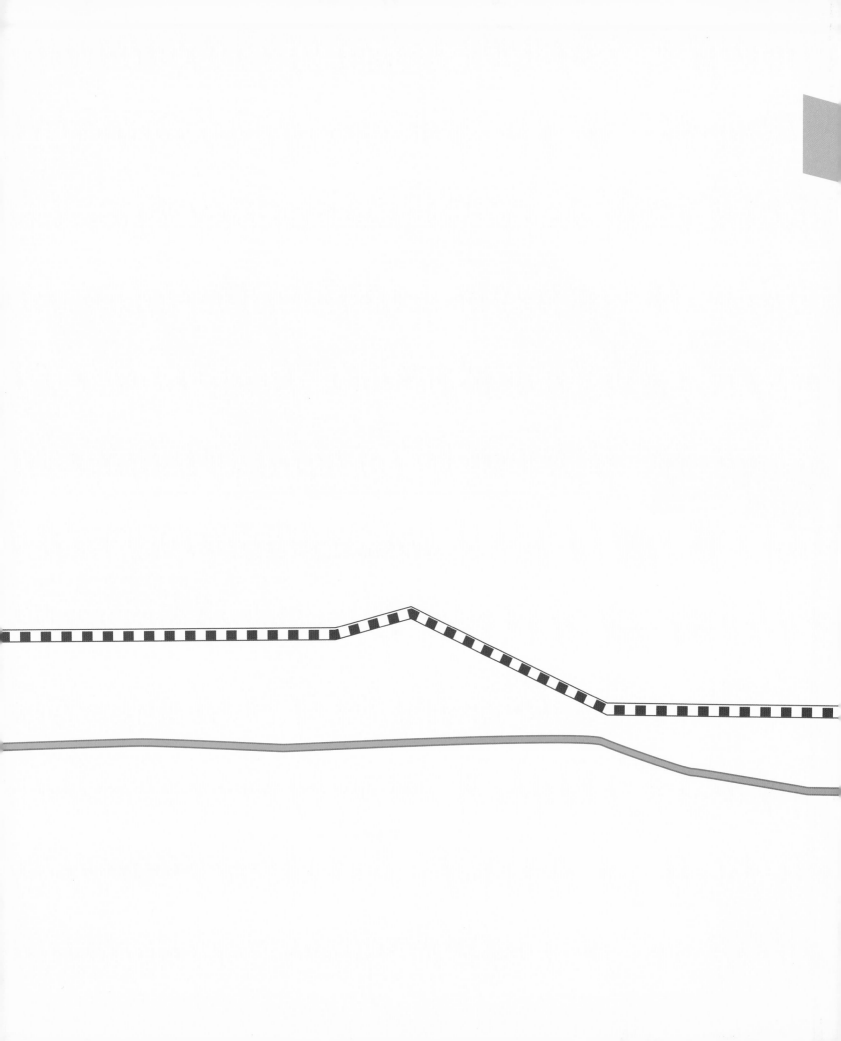

Barbecue Road Trip

Recipes, Restaurants, & Pitmasters from America's Great Barbecue

Michael Karl Witzel

CRESTLINE

DEDICATION

To the men and women who have raised barbecue to mythical proportions: America's pitmasters. For our culinary enjoyment, they spend countless hours toiling and sweating over smoking hot pits and stoking wood-fired ovens, lovingly tending to pork shoulders, butts, brisket, chicken, ribs, mutton, and more, nurturing them to a level of tenderness and smoky flavor unmatched by any other food consumed by man. Through a fusion of hard-learned cooking techniques, culinary intuition, and personal artistry, they transform what would otherwise be ordinary cuts of meat into extraordinary fare, providing the aficionado and casual diner alike with one of the tastiest genres of American food: Bar-B-Q.

This edition published in 2012 by
CRESTLINE
a division of BOOK SALES, Inc.
276 Fifth Avenue Suite 206
New York, New York 10001
USA

This edition published by arrangement with Voyageur Press an imprint of MBI Publishing Company.

First published in 2008 by Voyageur Press, an imprint of MBI Publishing Company, 400 First Avenue North, Suite 300, Minneapolis, MN 55401 USA

Witzel, Michael Karl, 1960-
  Barbecue road trip : recipes, restaurants, & pitmasters
  from America's great barbecue regions /
  by Michael Karl Witzel. -- 1st ed.
    p. cm.
  ISBN: 978-0-7858-2916-4
  1. Barbecue cookery--United States. I. Title.
  TX840.B3W58 2008
  641.7'6--dc22

                    2008001845

Editor: Dennis Pernu
Interior design: John Burnett/4 Eyes Design
Layout: Christopher Fayers

Printed in China

Front cover: Glowing neon greets customers at Corky's BBQ on busy Poplar Avenue in Memphis. *2008 Michael Karl Witzel*

Frontispiece: Bridges Barbecue Lodge, Shelby, North Carolina. *©2008 Michael Karl Witzel*

Contents: At Spring Creek Barbeque in Arlington, Texas, the razzle-dazzle of Las Vegas meets the small-town mystique of the Texas barbecue shack. Opened in 1980, it holds its own in a competitive market of surrounding eateries and boasts 24 locations in the Lone Star State. *2008 Michael Karl Witzel*

Back cover: Delicacies from America's four great 'cue regions, clockwise from top left: Kreuz Market, Lockhart, Texas. *©2008 Coolstock/Photo by Nicole Mlakar*; Corky's Ribs & BBQ, Memphis, Tennessee. *©Michael Karl Witzel*; Fiorella's Jack Stack, Martin City, Missouri. *©Michael Karl Witzel*; and Lexington's Bar-B-Q Center, North Carolina, *©2008 Michael Karl Witzel*.

Maps on pages 10, 52, 90, and 136: *©iStockphoto/Jami Garrisou*

Please note that these recipes have not been kitchen-tested. Many were converted for home use from restaurant-quantity recipes and may vary significantly from their restaurant versions. However, in most instances they will be a close approximation of the real thing. In other instances, recipes provided by restaurants were specifically designed for home preparation and for that reason, will not be comparable to items served at the restaurant itself. The source of each recipe is provided.

CONTENTS

ACKNOWLEDGMENTS

Bridges Barbecue Lodge, Shelby, North Carolina.
©2008 Michael Karl Witzel

WITHOUT THE ASSISTANCE OF THE ESTABLISHMENTS featured in this book, this inside look at America's four regions of barbecue would not have been possible.

Thank you to all the joints, grease houses, and restaurants who participated: A&R Bar-B-Que, The Bar-B-Q Shop, the Bar-B-Q Center, Arthur Bryant's Barbecue, Black's BBQ, Bridges Barbecue Lodge, Carolina Bar-B-Q, CD's Pit Bar-B-Q, Corky's Ribs & BBQ, Fiorella's Jack Stack Barbecue, Gates Bar-B-Q, Hayward's Pit Bar B Que, Interstate Bar-B-Que, Kreuz Market, Lazy-T Bar-B-Q, Leonard's Pit Barbecue, Lexington Barbecue, Little Pigs of America Barbecue, Luling City Market, Marlowe's Ribs & Restaurant, Pappa's World Famous Bar-B-Q, Parker's Barbecue, Payne's Bar-BQ, Railroad B-B-Q, Charles Vergos' Rendezvous, Roadhouse B-B-Q, Ronnie's B-B-Q, Rosedale Bar-B-Q, Rudy's Country Store & Bar-B-Q, The Salt Lick, Sammie's Bar-B-Q, Smitty's Market, The Smoke Shack Bar-B-Q, Spring Creek Barbeque, the Skylight Inn, Tarheel Q, Three Little Pigs Bar-B-Q, Tops Bar-B-Q, and Wilber's Barbecue.

Additional thanks go out to all of the individuals connected with these barbecue restaurants, including Gary Adams, Sharon Albright, Robert Mr. Shotgun Anderson, Michael Aycock, Bobby Battle, Gary Berbiglia, Richard Berrier, Edgar Black, Norma Black, Terry Black, Lyntoy Brandon, Debbie Bridges-Webb, Elliot Brooks, Dan Brown, Darrell Buchanan, Joe Capello, James Capo, Namon Carlton, Travis Carpenter, Pete Castillo, Rudy Castillo, Brian Channel, Melissa "Missy" Coleman, Cecil Conrad, Michael Conrad, Nancy Conrad, Sonny Conrad, Alan Cooper, Russ Craver, Sergio Darcia, Monique Davis, Pat Donohue, Case Dorman, David Dunn, Eddie Echols, Efrem Echols, Lisa Elliott, Aaron Ellis, Bobby Ellis, Vince Franz, John Fullilove, Gay Gaillard, Arzelia Gates, Ollie Gates, Paul Gattuso, Jay Gibbs, James Goodwin, Gerri Grady, J. J. Grady, Steve Grady, Robert Green, John Guerrero, Chris Hammond, Stacey Haywood, Dale Hipson, James Hokes, Diann Holiday, Jeremy Hollin, Ella Hope, James Howell, Tina Jennings, Bruce Jones, Jeff Jones, Pete Jones, Samuel Jones, Rita Kersey, John Kitchen, Tommy Kupczyk, Kevin Lamm, Clarence Lewis, Eric Lippard, Pedro Galvan Lopez, Claude Mann, Juan Martinez, Don Mclemore, Gene Medlin, Linda Medlin, Karen Miller, Nancy Monk, Rick Monk, Wayne Monk, Julie Monk Lopp, Henry Morris, Robert Moye, Angie Murdock, Jim Neely, Kenneth Neely, Kenneth Nickle, Chris Nielson, Anita Patrick, Barry Pelts, Donald Pelts, Roy Perez, Charles Perry, Bonnie Phifer, Eddie Radford, Michelle Ramos, Chase Ramsey, Natalie Ramsey, Parker Ramsey, Kelly Rhea, Terry Rhea, Tammy Rhodes, Scott Roberts, Charlie Robertson, Frankie Rodriquez, Roy Rosser, Jeff Rousselo, Jesse Salas, Lupe Salazar, Phillip Schenck, Keith Schmidt, Rick Schmidt, Jim Sells, Nina Sells, Kelly Shepard, Wilber Shirley, Marisha Smith, Wanda Smith, Hattie Spears, Hayward Spears, Steve Stolks, Marie Taylor, John Tetter, Ella Townes, Connie Trent, Ignacio Vaca, John Vergos, Nick Vergos, Eric Vernon, Frank Vernon, Hazelteen Vernon, Caylen Wall, Shannon Walsh, Curtis Waycaster, Bill Wendt, Cara Weston, Lyndell Whitmore, Edward Wicks, Donald Williams, Keith Wright, Kelly Wright, and Gorkem Yamandag.

Finally, a personal thank you to everyone else who assisted locally and behind the scenes, namely, office assistant Christina McKinney, photographer Nicole Mlakar-Livingston, and writer Gyvel Young-Witzel. If anyone was omitted from these acknowledgments, I offer my sincerest apologies. Please know that your assistance was important and your contribution to this effort invaluable. Thank you to all.

71

INTRODUCTION

WITH THE ADVENT OF TELEVISION NETWORKS devoted to foods and programs geared toward "cooking it yourself," today's backyard chefs consider themselves masters of the so-called "barbecue arts." Unfortunately, clothed in their "Kiss the Cook" aprons—with tongs in hand and battery-powered temperature probe at the ready—they are ill-prepared when it comes to duplicating real barbecue cooking.

You see, contrary to popular belief, barbecue isn't simply a matter of dousing a bag full of charcoal briquettes with lighter fluid, lighting a match, and then searing a slab of meat on a metal grill suspended above the glowing embers. Really, barbecuing isn't cooking in a sense that we know it at all, but rather a slow-smoking process that takes place over burned hardwoods like hickory or oak. It's the succulent smoke that prepares the meat for consumption and gives it character. And no—barbecue isn't cooking over a propane grill, either.

By all historical accounts, it appears that the confusion began in a land long ago and far away with a Haitian framework of sticks that was used for drying or roasting meat. Supposedly, the explorer Cortez and his happy-go-lucky band of pillagers were cruising the Caribbean when they encountered native Indians preparing fish on these racks of interwoven branches. As seafarers are apt to be, the band was very hungry and lavished praise and approval upon this curious method of meat preparation as their stomachs filled.

Consequently, they took the technique and the word to describe it with them. While their exploration skills were *nonpareil*, linguists they were not. As often happens, the pronunciation of their newly learned word changed gradually. In the Spanish tongue, the racks and the method of cooking came to be known by the word "barbacoa." After some further dilution over the passage of time, the word "barbecue" surfaced in English.

Unfortunately, the term did not distinguish the nuances involved in the cooking process and was soon adopted by anyone and everyone who cooked meat on a grill raised over a flaming heat source. By the time the backyard barbecue emerged as an American icon during the 1950s, people assumed that quickly cooking meat on a grill was barbecue. Soon, everything was fair barbecue game, including hamburgers, hot dogs, steaks—even sliced pineapple. By golly, if you could slap it on the grill and cook it without having it fall through the thin wire mesh and burn to a crisp, it was barbecue.

Despite the fact that the elements used to prepare old-fashioned, southern-smoked barbecue (of the type described in this book) and grilled foods have much in common, there are two subtle differences that should be noted in the two forms of cooking. First, with grilling, the fire—whether it uses wood coals or a gas flame for fuel—is very hot. Second, the foods that are placed upon the dancing flames are seared and cooked quickly. The desire to impart the meat with smoke flavor is secondary. Grilling is a lot like driving on the freeway: you can get there pretty fast, but you don't experience much of the journey while en route.

On the other hand, the type of smoking that is done in a covered cooking arrangement or barbecue "pit" relies on a more patient technique. Here, there are never any active flames directly under the meat. The cooking temperature is much lower and moisture is abundant, with the aroma of smoke a much desired part of the process. The meat is basted sparingly and cooked throughout. Time is of the essence, but not the way you would normally think: it takes 8 to 12 hours to cook the typical pork shoulder. There is no rush.

The resulting fall-off-the-bone-tender meat is what author John Egerton describes in *Southern Food* as a "moist, tender, delicious, and distinctively original delicacy." This is the back-road, slow-lane school of cooking, with all the delightful nuances of the cooking journey recorded in the meat itself.

Today, this time-honored path of slow-cooking is the route taken by barbecue fans in all 50 states. The gospel of 'cue has spread nationwide, with hand-me-down recipes and techniques exported from the South to all parts of the country—and new ones invented. The variety is lip-smacking to say the least.

In St. Louis, you may sample the best of barbecue pork steaks or pork spareribs. In Hawaii, you will find the traditional Asian-inspired plate lunch or "Hawaiian barbecue," with Emu-cooked (pit-cooked) pork butt (kalua pig) as the main ingredient. Up in Alaska, barbecued salmon—smoked the traditional way on cedar sticks—is a hands-down favorite. Down in Alabama, you might very well be surprised when your barbecue meat is served with "white sauce," a local favorite. In Arkansas, the prevalence of chicken dominates the menu, prepared with a dry rub and smoked (diners add their own sauce).

And it continues: Georgia can be categorized as a melting pot of regional variations where almost any type of barbecue sauce or cooking style can be found. Meanwhile, the state of Kentucky presents its own version of barbecued mutton doused with western Kentucky barbecue sauce or what the locals call "black dip," made with bourbon. Santa Maria, California, calls their town "The Barbecue Capital of the World" and serves up a copyrighted recipe of beef tri-tip roast—a boneless cut from the bottom sirloin that's cooked over coastal red oak. The fact is that coast-to-coast, nationwide, wherever you find meat, you will find an expert pitmaster or backyard wannabe stoking the coals in preparation.

But like the distinctive barbecue smoke ring—that bright pink colored, ⅛-inch layer that appears below the surface of the meat after cooking—there is a notable concentration of barbecue styles in one particular area of the United States. That area happens to be divided into what some refer to as the "four regions of barbecue," lauded by barbecue elite and laymen alike as the true bastions of authentic American 'cue.

For hardcore fans of smoked meat, no place can compare to Texas, Kansas City (Missouri), Memphis (Tennessee), or North Carolina. These are the four regions that set the standard for the nation. Here, the delineation between the types of meats, the time spent cooking it, the equipment and fuel used for cooking, the role of smoke in the preparation, the blend of seasonings, the style of serving, the type of side orders served, and the varieties of barbecue sauces and other flavorings used are the most distinct.

Throughout this geographical smoke ring of barbecue regions, one common denominator cuts across all social and economic lines, summed up most eloquently by Jeff Jones of the Skylight Inn of Ayden, North Carolina. As he puts it, "The particular barbecue that you take a liking to is according to whatever you grew up with! If you had barbecue with a lot of sauce, then you are going to want a lot of sauce on your barbecue. But if you grew up around these parts and are used to adding only a simple sauce made with vinegar and spices, that will be your favorite."

On the other hand, it can also be argued that "there ain't no such thing as bad barbecue—only good barbecue and better barbecue!" All preferences aside, the true, fanatical devotee of barbecue is hard-pressed to refuse any platter served to him or her, regardless of how or where it was prepared.

And that, my barbecue-loving friends, ties into your mission: get a true picture for yourself of what kind of barbecue is simply adequate and what kind of barbecue may be categorized as legendary. Head out on the highway and visit the pits of Texas, Kansas City, Memphis, and North Carolina

for yourself! Meet the real people who make the food, go behind the scenes, talk to the locals, and revel in the atmosphere.

Take your time—this isn't fast food that can be snatched up at a drive-thru window, but rather true American "slow food" that should be savored and enjoyed without haste. As you bite into a rack of succulent ribs, sink your teeth into perfectly smoked burnt ends, or wolf down a Lexington-style chopped-pork sandwich with brown, you'll discover your own favorites, your own legends.

Go there with a good appetite and take no heed to the reviews you may read online or in other publications. This author has discovered first-hand that when someone dismisses one of the classic pits as "not that good anymore," it's most often done out of some ulterior motive. I'm reminded of something Anita Patrick, long-time waitress at Corky's Bar-B-Q in Memphis, told me when I mentioned to her that I read her eatery was "overrated." "Jealousy is an ugly thing!" she exclaimed with great emotion, and I soon knew for myself that it was true. After sampling one of Corky's signature pulled-pork sandwiches piled high with coleslaw, I knew that I had found barbecue heaven.

For this reason and many more, I will make no attempts to rate one barbecue establishment over another or to convince you why one type or style of barbecue is superior. To do so would be presumptuous and require a certain amount of hubris on my part. I'll leave that unenviable task to the unending

roster of food and restaurant reviewers. Within the pages of this book, my goal is to introduce you to America's four most prominent regions of barbecue and leave you to make up your own mind as to what is good, better, and ultimately best.

So, if you claim to be a barbecue lover, it's your responsibility to seek out the grease houses of Kansas City and the classic barbecue pits of Memphis. It's your duty to amble on down to Texas for a bold taste of pit-smoked beef, and to mosey on over to North Carolina to experience the art of pig pickin' at its

In 1871, outdoor barbecue in New York City meant taking an entire ox and roasting it over coals on a hand-cranked spit. Picnic at the Brennan Societies, Lion Park, August 22. *From* Frank Leslie's Illustrated Newspaper, *author's collection*

finest. Whether you call it barbecue, bar-be-que, bar-b-q, bar-b-que, B-B-Q, BBQ, barbeque, or just plain 'cue, there's a style out there that will make your taste buds sing for joy and your spirit shout "hallelujah!" For this ecstasy is what makes up the myth—and the magic—of legendary barbecue.

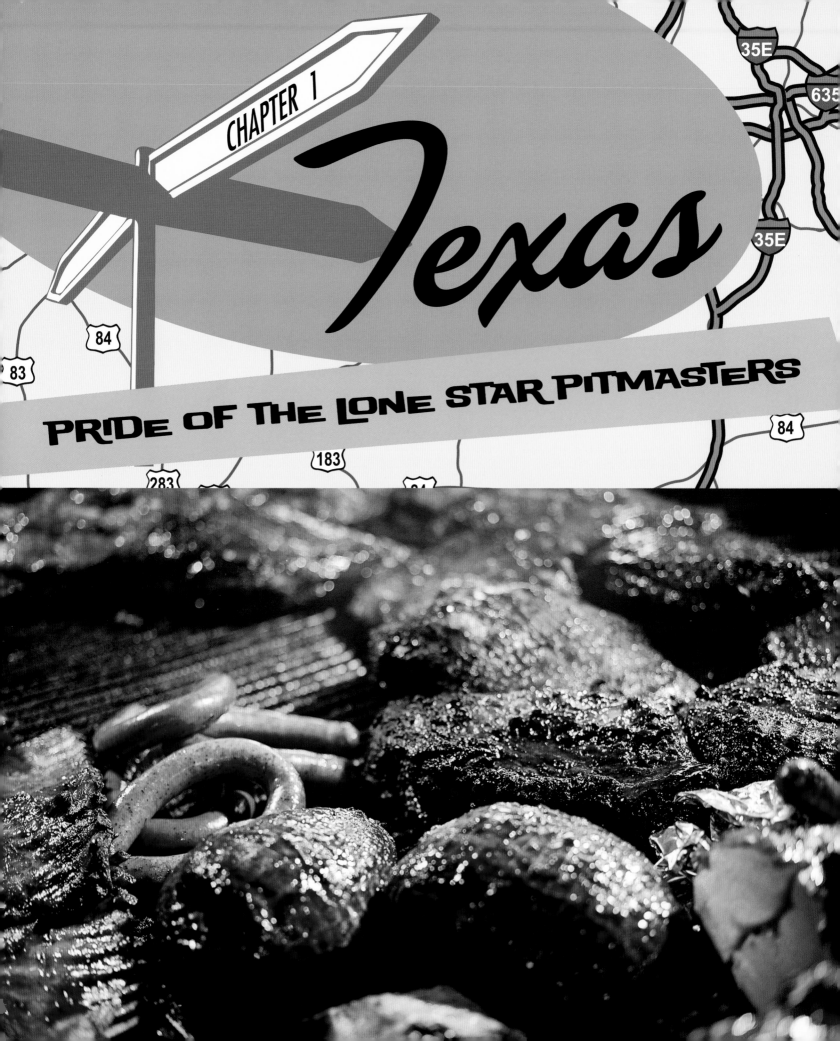

CHAPTER 1

Texas

PRiDE OF THE LONE STAR PiTMASTERS

ONE HUNDRED MILES SOUTH of Fort Worth, Texas, I'm traveling Highway 281 with the top down, exploring the Texas Hill Country in search of legendary American barbecue joints. I've sampled the wares of stainless-steel diners in the Northeast, supped at the greasy spoons of New Jersey, filled my belly at the chicken shack restaurants of the South, and reached for antacids at holes-in-the-wall out West. Now, I'm searching for barbecue joints and legend and lore that go along with them.

In the wavy currents of heat rising up from the road, my mind paints beautiful visions of smoked brisket, barbecue sauce, and beans. Rolling through quaint, one-stoplight towns like Glen Rose, Hamilton, and Hico, I pass farms and fields thick with carpets of bluebonnets and native wildflowers. This is the land first inhabited by Native Americans and later German settlers who ventured here to brave the heat and carve out a new life.

Hypnotized by the center stripe, the veil of modern life falls away and suddenly I'm viewing this road as a dirt trail, occupied by horse and buggy, cowboys and cattle, back during a time when roadside food meant cooking it yourself on the open range. I'm reminded of the history of this region and the debate that still rages among the learned Bubbas, Billy Bobs, and Bobbi-Jos as to the origins of this culinary form known as

Above: For hungry Hill Country travelers taking Highway 281 north into Lampasas, the Roadhouse BBQ is a welcome sight. Many such establishments are found along the less-traveled highways and byways, revealing their delights to those searching for culinary adventure. *©2008 Michael Karl Witzel*

Below: Inside the pit room at Kreuz Market, long brick pits with heavy, counterweighted metal lids are used to cook the meat indirectly. An open fire at the end of each long pit burns seasoned post oak. The flames are stoked around the clock. *©2008 Coolstock/Photo by Nicole Mlakar*

Opposite: For those standing in line and waiting for their table at The Salt Lick, the large circular pit becomes the main attraction, hypnotizing onlookers with its golden hues and promise of succulent flavor. *©2008 Coolstock/Photo by Nicole Mlakar*

Right: Cowboys didn't always dine on steak. The southern states' roundup wagons had a dish called S.O.B. No one but a dyed-in-the-wool south Texan could eat it at first try. Cooked as a stew and salted to taste, it was made from a short yearling. The small intestines, along with marrow, gut, heart, and liver were chopped into pieces with tallow and bits of beef thrown in. Chili powder was added until it was blazing hot and ready to eat. *Author's collection*

Below: When the lunch rush hits at Luling's City Market, each member of the barbecue team jumps into action. While one person takes orders, another slices meat while yet another makes sure the meat isn't overcooked. *©2008 Coolstock/Photo by Nicole Mlakar*

John Guerrero takes a break from carving meat to load one of the many pits at Kreuz Market with rings of savory sausage. Customers can buy vacuum-packed flats of these links in the adjoining shop and take them home. ©2008 Coolstock/Photo by Nicole Mlakar

barbecue. Some of the graybeards that I've talked to have spun tall tales of every description—something that a Texan has a right to do—including the story that barbecue is native-born and got its start in the Lone Star State.

As I'm told, it began long, long before I was even knee-high to a grasshopper, way back before there was any practical refrigeration, specifically the period between 1830 and 1890. This was the era of great European immigration in central Texas and the arrival of German and Czech butchers who brought with them their Old World methods of smoking meats. As they had done back home, the immigrants sold their fresh meat in a market and smoked the leftovers in smokers out back.

In those days, an itinerant clientele of black and Hispanic cotton pickers simply couldn't get enough of the smoked pork loin and sausage sold in these markets. Much like today's portable fast food meal, no sooner had they purchased the meat than they set upon eating it—directly from the butcher paper it came wrapped in. For the migrants, this was regarded as "barbecue," much to the astonishment of the butchers.

In 1850, European immigrants made up more than 5 percent of the Texas population. Now, more than 158 years later, their way of life has left a lasting impression on Texas

Above: The service arrangement at Black's is basic: meat comes off the pit, is sliced on butcher-block tables, and is served to customers waiting at the counter. There's no mystery here: you know exactly where your food is coming from and how it's prepared. *©2008 Coolstock/Photo by Nicole Mlakar*

Right: In 1935, Hugh and Grace Hiett ran this barbecue joint in Houston, Texas, offering customers "Plantation Pit" barbecue. Even in Texas, the proprietors of barbecue shacks looked to the Old South for their culinary inspiration. *Author's collection*

Right: At Kreuz Market, when you're hungry and ready to eat, there is nothing quite as enticing as your order of meat (sausage and brisket shown here) as it is placed on a pristine piece of butcher paper on the counter in front of you. *©2008 Coolstock/Photo by Nicole Mlakar*

Below: Underwood's began during the Great Depression of the 1930s when Brady, Texas, butcher M. E. Underwood began cooking and selling barbecue door-to-door. By the 1940s, he had a white frame shack by the road and opened the first in a chain of 30 (this location was on old Route 66 in Amarillo, Texas). *Author's collection*

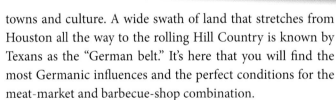

towns and culture. A wide swath of land that stretches from Houston all the way to the rolling Hill Country is known by Texans as the "German belt." It's here that you will find the most Germanic influences and the perfect conditions for the meat-market and barbecue-shop combination.

On the other hand, I've heard other histories, too, stating that African-Americans brought the tradition of barbecue with them from the South. These food historians say that the process started during the 1850s, after Texas joined the Union as a slave state in 1845. With its wide-open spaces and affordable land prices, the cotton planters of the South eyeballed the Texas region as an ideal place to set up shop.

In short order, farmers from North Carolina, South Carolina, Alabama, and Mississippi moved in to take advantage of the bargains. Of course, wealthy plantation owners brought

Established in 1932, Black's BBQ continues to prepare the same fare that has been wowing Lockhart customers since the early days, including barbecue brisket, chicken, sausage, ribs, and more. Big Red—with a taste a lot like bubble gum—is a local favorite. Created by mixing orange and lemon oils with the traditional vanilla used in other cream sodas, it's a popular soda pop in the Texas market. ©2008 Coolstock/Photo by Nicole Mlakar

their slave families with them, some with hundreds of servants. After slavery was abolished in 1865, the cooking styles of these freemen gained popularity outside of the plantations. The ability of African-American workers to take what some viewed as inferior cuts of meat and turn them into mouth-watering fare—as if by culinary alchemy—became widely known in East Texas and beyond.

And what of the early Anglo cowboys and Mexican *vaqueros* of the 1800s who claim they established this form of cooking? As still other historians report, these early riders of the range cooked game like rabbit, squirrel, and venison in open pits. Along the Rio Grande Valley, some followed the traditions of Mexico and wrapped their meat in maguey leaves. Encased in this protective wrapper, they buried it in burning coals where it cooked for hours. Using this Mexican technique of *barbacoa*, the finished meat emerged from the pit so tender that it would make a grown man cry.

THE SALT LICK, DRIFTWOOD As I pass through Marble Falls, Johnson City, Blanco, and Wimberley, I'm pushing the speed limit: the locals all know that barbecue joints 'round here never have an unlimited supply of meat. In fact, it's best to arrive early if you want to eat. When a popular pit runs out of barbecue in Texas, they really mean it. No amount of begging will get you some unless you happen to be the owner's bird dog or a blood relation (even then, it's quite possible that you will go home hungry).

But that's not what happens at The Salt Lick, a Texas treasure located off FM (farm-to-market) Road 1826 in Driftwood, Texas. The rock building that houses the restaurant sits on land owned by the Roberts family for more than a hundred years. In fact, Salt Lick founder Thurman Roberts was born on this very tract of land in 1909. His kinfolk came to Driftwood in 1867 from Georgia, South Carolina, and northern Mississippi by wagon train.

Right: Manager and pitmaster Joe Capello oversees the activities at Luling's City Market. Here, it's all about the meat: smoking, it, slicing it, and serving it. ©2008 Coolstock/ Photo by Nicole Mlakar

Below: At City Market, the brick pit with its heavy steel door reminds those who dare to duplicate this kind of barbecue at home that this is no game for the amateur. Here are the tools of the pitmaster's trade: a shovel for manipulating hot coals, a steel poker to stoke the embers, and a pile of seasoned wood. ©2008 Coolstock/Photo by Nicole Mlakar

Along the way, the clan cooked over a large open fire surrounded by rocks, the tradition of the day. On top of the rocks, they fitted a large metal grill, elevated off the ground. On this, they cooked whatever game they could catch, searing the meat directly over the heat and then moving it farther down the grill to continue cooking over indirect heat. Around one side of the fire an earthen berm held in the heat and the smoke.

In the Roberts family, this became the traditional cooking method passed down from one generation to the next. One day Thurman and his wife Hisako decided to take tradition one step further. They wanted to live *and* work in Driftwood and devised a method to make a living, one that would involve the whole family. In 1967, Thurman and his son Scott strolled down to the pasture and marked off the ground with his boot. That mark became the center of the Salt Lick barbecue pit and the beginning of a Texas legend.

In 1969, the family built a structure around the circular pit out of limestone rocks quarried from the ranch. For the interior of the building, they used recycled wood culled from old barns on the property. When it was finished, the small

Above: The Salt Lick ships their barbecued meats and sauces to transplanted Texans and aficionados nationwide, but to experience the real atmosphere of the joint, it's best to visit in person. ©2008 Michael Karl Witzel

Opposite above: A throwback to the days of the early West, the circular Salt Lick finishing pit is where all the meat goes for final tender loving care before it's served. Real wood fires the pit, and a dedicated pitmaster bastes the delectables with sauce. ©2008 Coolstock/Photo by Nicole Mlakar

Opposite below: The Maillard reaction is one of cooking's great miracles. This chemical reaction between amino acids and sugars is created by heat and responsible for the crust on breads, dark beer, and turning the outside of roasted meat into something rich and complex. By keeping the heat under 275 degrees Fahrenheit and cooking slowly, the fats and collagens melt, making meats like The Salt Lick's famous barbecue brisket juicy and flavorful. ©2008 Michael Karl Witzel

restaurant operated without running water or electricity and seated only a dozen customers. For the first two years, the going was tough.

But changes came quickly. Since that time, the Roberts expanded the restaurant three times. Today, the homestead includes an outdoor seating space known as the "Rock Patio," along with several big banquet rooms. With its cone-shaped exhaust hood and wood-fired heat supply, The Salt

The Salt Lick's Smoked Pork Spareribs

1 rack natural pork spare ribs (13 ribs)
Salt Lick Dry Rub (salt, black pepper, cayenne)
Salt Lick BBQ Sauce (no tomatoes)

With a clean, dry cloth, remove the excess moisture from the surface of the ribs. Apply dry rub evenly, coating the entire surface of the ribs just before cooking (if you put the rub on early, it will pull the moisture out of the meat). Sear over direct heat until caramelized. This is key. Remove to indirect heat. Baste with Salt Lick BBQ Sauce. Place the ribs, bone side up, in a 250-degree smoker for 3 to 3-1/2 hours. Turn and baste with sauce at least twice.

Serves: 3-4

Notes: Scott Roberts buys spareribs, 4.2 pounds or less, "natural fall," which means the brisket bone is still attached. He removes that bone and uses it to flavor beans. Unlike many barbecuers, he does not remove the membrane on the back of the ribs before cooking. He thinks it keeps the meat moister.

SOURCE: SCOTT ROBERTS, THE SALT LICK, DRIFTWOOD, TEXAS

Lick's circular indoor finishing pit remains the centerpiece. From the Hill Country to the Piney Woods, you won't see anything else like it.

Fortunately, I have arrived early enough to stake my personal claim to a plate of barbecue. It's 9:30 a.m. and the circular pit is already hot, stoked with glowing logs and heaped high with the sumptuous colors of briskets, ribs, and sausage (the initial smoking is done in a large barbecue oven in back). As the pit boss circles the pit, he reaches in and mops the meat with a generous dollop of sauce. The ritual is almost religious in its manifestation, a reverence for the meat evidenced by his careful attention. The gleaming delights tantalize the senses.

Although Texans may be found barbecuing pork, cuts of steak, and even the occasional cow's head, brisket is probably the most popular cut. These days, it's one of The Salt Lick's specialties and Scott Roberts (the son of the original founders, Thurman and Hisako) doesn't mind sharing his insider secrets with the public. Barbecue is in his blood and he loves to cook, sometimes holding classes at the Central Markets in Texas.

"Our briskets are bigger and thicker," says Roberts, "a specialty item from a supplier in Kansas." Before hitting the fire, the meat is sprinkled with a dry rub consisting of salt, black pepper, and cayenne pepper in a ratio of 2:1:1. Then, the brisket is seared fat side down on direct heat. The sauce is mopped onto the meat side to form a moisture barrier. The result is a moist, delicate flavor with just the right hint of smoke. "We adhere to the traditions taught to us by my father and his ancestors," he adds. "He always started with a quality piece of meat and was sure that he ended up with a quality product."

Scott's father also established the tradition of using live oak, a wood that adds a bold, aromatic flavor to the meat. In many parts of the Lone Star State, oak and pecan are favorites for smoking. But there's also mesquite. Abundant in South and West Texas, it lends a distinctive, sharp taste to the meat that can turn bitter if it's cooked for too long. In East Texas (and

Rudy Castillo opens the lid to one of the many barbecue pits at City Market to check on racks of sausage links. The heavily encrusted interior of the lid is seasoned with years of use, contributing to the quality of the finished product like no bottle of liquid smoke ever could. ©2008 Coolstock/Photo by Nicole Mlakar

Brisket, sausage, beans, coleslaw, and potato salad are staples at The Salt Lick, along with specially baked bread loaves. At most of the other Texas joints, it's store-bought white bread or Texas toast—straight from the bag. ©2008 Michael Karl Witzel

The Salt Lick's Smoked BBQ Brisket

8–10 pounds grain-fed brisket (recommended: Angus beef)
3 tablespoons Salt Lick Dry Rub
Salt Lick BBQ Sauce (no tomatoes)

With a clean, dry cloth, remove the excess moisture from the surface of the brisket. Apply the dry rub evenly, coating the entire brisket. Cook over oak or oak charcoal. Cook brisket fat side down above the coals. Sear both sides over direct heat until caramelized, about 5 to 10 minutes on each side. Baste both sides with Salt Lick BBQ Sauce (do not use any tomato-based barbecue sauce as this will burn and leave a bitter taste).

Move brisket to a 190-degree smoker (use oak wood to smoke, not mesquite), cooking in indirect heat. Cook meat side up for about 16 hours or until the internal temperature at the thickest part is 165 degrees (insert meat thermometer into center of side, but in muscle, not fat). Baste and mop the meat side only, at least four times during the cooking process to form a moisture barrier. Slice to order.

Feeds: 8–10 people.

SOURCE: SCOTT ROBERTS, THE SALT LICK, DRIFTWOOD, TEXAS

Basting meat with barbecue sauce or another liquid concoction is one technique that pitmaster Juan Martinez uses to keep the meat moist while cooking. However, the sauce at The Salt Lick differs in that its lack of tomatoes allows it to caramelize, forming a crust that seals in the juices.
©2008 Coolstock/Photo by Nicole Mlakar

throughout the other barbecue regions of the South), hickory is the most popular wood, providing a mellow, smoked flavor that many of the old-time pitmasters swear by. But not every Texas region is blessed with ample supplies. Up in the panhandle near El Paso, the pit bosses must have all their wood shipped in.

As the meat comes ever-closer to being ready to eat, the kitchen staff makes the final touches on the side dishes and desserts. First, they roll out racks of hot pecan pies, arranged in pretty rows. An original recipe of Thurman Roberts, their flaky crusts are still hand-rolled the old-fashioned way. While the pies cool, the staff slides trays of blackberry and peach

cobblers into the ovens to bake. With a wave of the hand and a wink of the eye, some of Driftwood's old-time residents gossip that Scott "borrowed" the cobbler recipe from a Mrs. Hall and Mrs. Echols. "You can probably say that the cobbler recipes are old Driftwood recipes," laughs Scott.

Scott explains that "cabbage and the potatoes are the stars in his two side dishes, potato salad and coleslaw." This means they are made fresh without mayonnaise and served in the traditional style. The list of ingredients is simple: cabbage mixed with a vinegar and oil dressing (no carrots, raisins, or celery seed). "The coleslaw is served immediately," says Scott. Otherwise, "the vinegar breaks down the cabbage and it loses the crunch." For the potato salad, a similar simplicity: potatoes are boiled inside their jackets, peeled, and cut. Add salt, pepper, pickled onion, and a dash of Salt Lick barbecue sauce, and you have a unique twist on an old Texas German recipe.

The French created pecan pie after they settled in New Orleans and Native Americans introduced them to the nut. It's sometimes referred to as "New Orleans pecan pie," adding an aura of French cuisine to a home-cooked comfort food. The makers of Karo syrup popularized the dish, and many recipes—even one credited to a well-known New Orleans restaurant—specify Karo syrup as an ingredient. At The Salt Lick, the pies are all homemade. *©2008 Coolstock/Photo by Nicole Mlakar*

In the Texas Hill Country, breaking bread at The Salt Lick is a weekend tradition. From all over the state, the devoted come to this sanctuary of barbecue to experience food that cannot be duplicated at home. *©2008 Coolstock/Photo by Nicole Mlakar*

Unlike many of today's restaurants, the public is privy to everything that happens to the meat before it is served at The Salt Lick. Eyeballing the glistening product is all part of the magic of dining there, whetting the appetite for the meal to come. Juan Martinez tends the pit. ©2008 Coolstock/ Photo by Nicole Mlakar

Salt Lick Style Rub

2 parts salt
1 part black pepper
1 part cayenne

Mix ingredients together in a bowl and rub on both sides of brisket at least one hour before cooking.

SOURCE: SCOTT ROBERTS, THE SALT LICK, DRIFTWOOD, TEXAS

But all this talk of cobbler and side orders is too much. I'm hungry and ready to sample the wares of this Texas landmark. Thankfully, I'm rewarded for my patience just a few moments later when the server lays down a "Family Style" order of 'cue complete with what the menu describes as "heaping helpings of beef, sausage, and pork ribs, served with potato salad, coleslaw, beans, bread, pickles, and onions." A tall glass of sweet iced tea is my beverage of choice. Lacking the carbonation of modern soft drinks, you can down it fast, its smooth finish the perfect thirst-quencher for smoked meat.

With little restraint, I dive into the brisket and my fondness grows. Next, I take a taste of the sausage and I grow more infatuated. Finally, I bite into the ribs and discover that I am in love. *Mi amor*, is it possible that great-tasting barbecue activates the same pleasure areas of the brain?

Just when I think it can't get any better, I pour on The Salt Lick's signature barbecue sauce. But this isn't the thick molasses- and tomato-based sauce that I'm used to. "Our sauce is more of a southeastern sauce that's become—for lack of a better word—'Texafied'," explains Roberts. "That means that over the years, some of the natural ingredients that are native to this area—like chili powder, cumin, and cayenne pepper— have found their way into our barbecue sauce recipe."

Not surprisingly, the credit for the formula goes to Scott's mom, Hisako Roberts. Although customers pour it on with great abandon, Scott says that it's in the pit area where the concoction really makes a difference. "Because the sauce has no tomatoes in it, it doesn't burn during the cooking process . . . so we use it to baste the meats," he explains. "It helps to hold the moisture in the meats but also has a high sugar-acidity content to it. Over the open pit it caramelizes on the outside of the meat and drips down into the coals. When it flares up, the essence of the sauce rises back up in the pit and gives the meat a unique flavor."

My appetite agrees with Scott's analysis. Methodically, I finish off my hunk of brisket and down the last drop of iced tea. Somehow, I manage to wolf down a piece of pecan pie and get another slice to go. I'm expected for a late lunch at my next 'cue joint, so I thank Scott Roberts for his hospitality and for sharing the traditions of The Salt Lick with me—and my belly.

Lupe Salazar adds the finishing touches to a barbecue plate. At The Salt Lick, the barbecue sauce is a highly desirable addition to the flavor palette, combining with the smoky finish of the meat to create a taste sensation otherwise unattainable alone. ©2008 Michael Karl Witzel

Right: Looking a lot like pieces of smoked meat, these counterweights for barbecue pit covers are attached to heavy steel cables and strung over pulleys, allowing the pitmaster to lift the heavy coverings with minimal effort. ©2008 Coolstock/Photo by Nicole Mlakar

Below: Special orders don't upset at Black's. Terry Black prepares an order of meat for a customer as his pitmaster and carver keep the barbecue machine running. ©2008 Coolstock/ Photo by Nicole Mlakar

SIDE ITEMS		SERVING	PINT	QUART
BEANS Seasoned Pinto Beans		1.35	2.65	5.35
CREAM CORN Rudy's Secret Recipe & a Guest Favorite		1.90	3.80	7.50
POTATO SALAD Fresh Potatoes in a Homestyle Dressing		1.35	2.65	5.35
OLE SLAW Creamy Homestyle Recipe		1.35	2.65	5.35
EACH COBBLER Fresh Peaches & Homemade Crust		2.15	4.30	8.60

DILL PICKLE		JALAPENO	ONION
.50 HALF	.95 WHOLE	.25	.25

While some Texas barbecue temples insist on carrying a minimum of side orders (if any), Rudy's offers a full range of sides and desserts. Many of the recipes were developed by Rudy's late barbecue guru, Doc Holiday. ©2008 Coolstock/Photo by Nicole Mlakar

On my way out, I weave through a packed house and meet the doleful gaze of the hopefuls waiting in line to get their share. Scott assured me that they don't run out of barbecue here at The Salt Lick, so there's really no need for anyone to worry. As I pass through the wrought-iron gates and get back out onto the main road, I think about how much I'm impressed by the rituals that have been kept alive here. Change can be good, but *not* when it comes to barbecue!

RUDY'S BAR-B-Q, LEON SPRINGS I stow my bottle of Salt Lick barbecue sauce, conjure a modest burp, and point my modern-day wagon south, weaving my way out through the farm-to-market roads. Ten miles west of San Antonio, I intend to sample more good eats at Rudy's Bar-B-Q in Leon Springs. Mapped out by an early Spanish explorer, the town's abundant springs were once vital to the survival of its residents, including local Indian tribes such as the Coahuiltacans, Tonkawas, and

Comanches. Today, water is of secondary importance—now it's barbecue sauce and Shiner Bock beer that ensure the survival of modern-day Texans.

Rudy's Country Store and Bar-B-Q wasn't always a chain with 16 locations. It actually began in 1929 as a modest one-pump gasoline station called "Rudolph's." The owner, Rudolph Aue, was the son of Leon Springs' founder and German immigrant Max Aue, who originally developed the land and founded the town. The elder Aue also served in the Texas Rangers, was a postmaster, and ran a general store, a stagecoach rest stop, and a hotel.

In 1989, Rudolph Aue sold the rural outpost to Florida restaurateur Phil Romano, who had already adopted Texas as his home. Romano was eager to build a restaurant chain around the mystique of barbecue and had the credentials to do so: both the Macaroni Grill and Fuddruckers restaurant concepts were his creations. In its rough form, he saw something unique in the Leon Springs store and believed he could take his brainstorm to new heights—Texas style.

From experience, Romano knew that his business would only be as good as the food that he served. Priority one was to find an expert who knew what he was doing when it came to fixing real authentic barbecue that would draw people in from the next county. So, Romano and his partners began asking around to see if anyone knew someone who could be their resident barbecue guru. More than once, the name that came up was "Doc Holiday."

At the time, Holiday was working at the Oak Hills Country Club near Austin as a bartender and dabbled in catering on the side. There, many club members talked about their hunting leases and the outdoor activities they were involved in. A few expressed interest in having better food while on their Texas safaris. One thing led to another and soon Doc was accompanying the local sportsmen on their outings and catering the whole affairs. Sometimes cooking under the most extreme conditions with minimal equipment and supplies, he proved his mettle and made quite a reputation for himself as a cook.

Doc's Roasted Potatoes

4 medium white potatoes
2 tablespoons Rudy's Rub
2 tablespoons cooking oil

Set oven at 350 degrees. Mix rub and oil in a bowl and set aside. Wash potatoes and dice in cubes about 1-inch thick. Blend potatoes in rub mixture. Place in a greased sheet pan. Roast in oven until golden brown, about 30 minutes.

Serves: 4–6

SOURCE: "DOC" HOLIDAY, RUDY'S COUNTRY STORE AND BAR-B-Q, LEON SPRINGS, TEXAS

Rudy's brick barbecue pits employ a fire chamber at one end, which provides the hot smoke that's drawn across the meat to cook it. This indirect method of cooking is difficult to duplicate at home, calling for the construction of specialized smokers much different than standard barbecue "grills." ©2008 Coolstock/Photo by Nicole Mlakar

Little did anyone know that cooking came easy for Doc. After all, he had a great teacher: his mother. From her, Holiday learned how to make everything from boiled eggs to brisket, later adding his own twist. During his elementary and junior high school years, he would come home from school and experiment in the kitchen. While most of the neighborhood kids were outside playing ball, Doc was in the kitchen basting brisket. No sooner was Holiday home and his books put up than his mother would call and give him instructions over the phone on how to cook dinner (she worked two jobs).

Besides the cooking, Holiday was also responsible for the long, narrow, wood-fired barbecue pits that are used at the Leon Springs location. He had the plans for their design drawn up and with a helper from San Antonio built the pits himself. Knowing when the meat was "just right" by eye, ear, and smell alone, he "tuned" the final configuration of the pits to cook perfect BBQ.

Rudy's director of marketing, Mr. Shannon Walsh, tells me that the Leon Springs location is unique because it uses what some people in Bexar County refer to as "German-style brick pits," where the fire is at one end and the smoke stack is at the other. "The pit draws the heat from the fire so that the smoke rolls over the top of the meat and then through the bottom and up into the smokestack," he explains. "We call that barbecuing, not smoking. Smoking would take about 15 to 16 hours, whereas we put the seasoning on our briskets the night before and then let them cook for 8 to 10 hours before we serve them."

After battling the traffic through "San Antone," I finally arrive in Leon Springs, finding it difficult to imagine how this all must have looked back in the 1800s. Senior manager

RUDY'S RUB $6.59

DOC'S NOTSAHOT SAUSE $5.45

32 OZ SAUSE $8.50

SAUSE BY THE CASE $90.00

Above: At Luling's City Market, the pits are fired at the back of a building in an area separated from the rest of the structure. The smoke is drawn from the firebox into the pits, where it cooks the meats in a long, slow process. ©2008 Coolstock/Photo by Nicole Mlakar

Above right: Rudy's is a strong believer in using barbecue sauce on their meat and is not ashamed of the various blends that they have for sale to the public. Readers of the *San Antonio Current* voted Rudy's the Best Barbecue of San Antonio in 2003. ©2008 Coolstock/Photo by Nicole Mlakar

Doc's Broccoli Cornbread

2 boxes Jiffy cornbread mix
4 eggs
1 (12-ounce) carton cottage cheese
1/2 teaspoon dill weed
1 (10-ounce) box frozen chopped broccoli, thawed
2 sticks butter, melted

Preheat oven to 400 degrees. Lightly butter 9x13 inch baking pan.

Combine cornbread mix, eggs and cottage cheese. Add dill weed, then broccoli and half of the butter. Stir, then add remaining butter. Pour mixture into pan, then smooth top of mixture with spatula. Bake until golden brown. Test doneness by putting toothpick in center of cornbread; it is ready when it comes out clean.

Makes: 12 servings

SOURCE: "DOC" HOLIDAY, RUDY'S COUNTRY STORE AND BAR-B-Q, LEON SPRINGS, TEXAS

Customers queue up to make their barbecue purchase at Rudy's, where an eclectic assortment of beer and soft drinks await them in an ice-filled cooler. *©2008 Coolstock/ Photo by Nicole Mlakar*

and 15-year veteran of barbecue cookery Stacey Haywood welcomes me and shows me the bustling operation. Haywood was Doc Holiday's right-hand man, privy to all his secrets. We begin to talk about his mentor's influence at Rudy's.

Holiday's knack in the kitchen and his enthusiasm were two key ingredients in the success of Rudy's. Until his death in 2007, partner Holiday was the cornerstone of the operation, teaching team members his barbecue secrets, developing new offerings like barbecue turkey, and inventing flavorful rubs like the ones currently used on Rudy's meats and poultry. He loved nothing more than to cook, invent new products, and see people enjoy his foods.

Rudy's ever popular "sause" was an original creation, too, inspired by one that was made by his mother and formulated one day when a Rudy's patron tried to put mustard on prime rib. Well, Holiday would have none of that, so he ran across the street to get a few items at the store. When he came back, he whipped up the sauce right there and then. After the other partners tasted it, they were making calls to get the stuff bottled. Today, it's shipped to barbecue sauce lovers around the world. I'm told that recently Rudy's shipped 35 one-gallon containers of its sauce on a C-5 transport to destinations in Baghdad, Kandahar, and Turkmenistan.

Walsh excitedly continues the Rudy's story where Haywood leaves off. "We take great pride in our military and all the great things they do," he announces. "For the last three years, right around Memorial Day, we have a 'Sauce for Soldiers' program

Right: The Rudy's location in Leon Springs commemorates the great flood of 1998 with a dining room wall mural. October of that year was the heaviest month for rainfall since 1871. Heavy rains caused creeks and rivers to overflow their banks, inundating the area with water. ©2008 Coolstock/Photo by Nicole Mlakar

Below: As William Allen White (1868–1944) wrote: "In the Barbecue is any four footed animal—be it mouse or mastodon—whose dressed carcass is roasted whole . . . at its best it is a fat steer, and must be eaten within an hour of when it is cooked. For if ever the sun rises upon Barbecue, its flavor vanishes like Cinderella's silks, and it becomes cold baked beef—staler in the chill dawn than illicit love." Just one of the reasons that City Market cooks it up slow—and serves it fast. Here, Aaron Ellis carves the meat. ©2008 Coolstock/Photo by Nicole Mlakar

BABY BACK   8.29 — 15.49
SAUSAGE
CHICKEN
SAUSE
NOTSAHOT SAUSE
RUDY'S RUB
GIFT CERTIFICATE

Above: At Rudy's in Leon Springs, customers young and old come for barbecue in the typical Texas meat market style. The meat is sold by the pound and wrapped in butcher paper. *©2008 Coolstock/Photo by Nicole Mlakar*

Opposite: Before they are placed into the pits for cooking, City Market's loosely packed sausage links are stored on a moveable rack (with wheels) in a refrigerated room. *©2008 Coolstock/Photo by Nicole Mlakar*

where we sell sauce and donate $2 for every bottle that's sold to the military. When it's all over, we give the proceeds to the wounded warriors who are stationed out of Brooks Army Medical Center, the unit off Fort Sam Air Force Base down in San Antonio. We take care of a lot of the injured soldiers down there and basically raised a total of $30,000 during the last couple of years just by selling Rudy's barbecue sauce for a couple of months!"

But whether they're military, civilian, young, old, local, or out-of-towner, it seems that everyone living or "just passing through" Texas loves to eat Rudy's barbecue. Every month,

Rudy's sells more than 100,000 pounds of brisket, the top-selling single menu item, accounting for 20 to 25 percent of sales. The number-two best-seller is turkey breast, followed by pork loin, chicken, ribs, and sausage (both regular and jalapeño). Each month, the company also sells more than 5,000 gallons of its signature "sause" (available in mildly fiery "Regular" or tame "Sissy" varieties), much of it via the Internet.

At Rudy's, the no-frills, slice-and-weigh-to-order meat-market-style dining that carries over from the old German traditions remains popular with the barbecue crowd. Pickles, onions, and sliced white bread are the traditional "go-withs," and Rudy's signature "sause" is served on the side. A la carte accompaniments such as "Rudy-ized" pinto beans—flavored with a secret blend of seasonings and spiked with sausage pieces—are world-class. You can even get jumbo smoked potatoes, coleslaw, and special recipe cream corn that's 100 percent Doc Holiday. Homespun dessert offerings include homemade banana or chocolate pudding and fruit cobbler.

Although an eclectic menu like this is more than adequate to explain the popularity of Texas barbecue, Walsh elaborates on why he thinks it's so popular. "It all comes down to the fact that barbecue is a comfort food. It's not elegant, you can roll your sleeves up with it, you can eat it on butcher paper, you can eat it with your fingers if you want to, and you can slather barbecue sauce on it," he states. "Barbecue is a comfort food that goes very, very well with family and with friends. And as you can see, people rally around it."

But Walsh is preaching to the choir. I'm already convinced of barbecue's popularity and appeal—especially after sampling some of Rudy's moist brisket doused in a profuse amount of their sauce. The exterior bark of the meat proves particularly tasty during this visit and I'm left completely satisfied with my lunchtime meal. But I still have more barbecue to sample.

I thank my hosts for their hospitality and refuel my ragtop at the pumps outside before I set out to leave. I chuckle at the funny Rudy's sign that brags this is the "Wurst Barbecue in Texas" and stow my doggy bag of sausages in the backseat cooler.

SMITTY'S MARKET, LOCKHART Back north up I-35, I branch off to the east, destined for what many regard as the nexus of Texas barbecue, the smoked utopia of 'cue, if you will, a little town called Lockhart that takes the genre of barbecue and elevates it to something beyond legendary.

A few hours later, I enter the city limits of Lockhart. Greeted by stately old homes and an inviting small-town charm, I'm impressed by the grandeur of the town square. At the center sits a large stone courthouse, delineated by four streets around. The arrangement recalls the state's Mexican roots, when the town square was the place to meet on market

days and people brought extra food and set up tables to sell baked goods and handmade wares. The courthouse came later when early settlers realized that meeting at the local saloon wasn't conducive to conducting legal business.

An assortment of retail shops and other businesses flank the courthouse. Smitty's Market is one of those businesses—the typical Texas meat market and barbecue joint, featuring a storefront that makes you think you stepped back in time, and an atmosphere that hollers "Main Street, America." It's named after Edgar "Smitty" Schmidt, the man who purchased the downtown market back in 1948.

I meet Nina Sells, Schmidt's daughter and current owner, who graciously gives me a tour of the local landmark. The first things that catch my eye are the massive barbecue pits. Their appearance is unlike anything else I have seen in the

Frankie Rodriquez and his associate, Aaron Ellis (left), prepare another order on the heavy butcher-block table at City Market. It's a serious operation: appetites are at stake, as well as the reputation of a Central Texas legend.
©2008 Coolstock/Photo by Nicole Mlakar

Jim Sells runs Smitty's Market with his wife, Nina Schmidt Sells. His role in the business is hands-on: tending to the pits, slicing meat, and making sure that the customers are happy. ©2008 Coolstock/Photo by Nicole Mlakar

strip mall joints and franchised chain stores of the big cities. The high-market ceilings and brick walls are encrusted with a thick layer of soot, too. The smoky coating is everywhere in the pit-area anteroom, painting the interior with a unique barbecue patina.

Built from red brick, the oversized pits are outfitted with counterweighted lids and fired with real wood—smoking, burning logs that rest in glowing piles at the end of the pits in a firebox area. They take a lot of wood. Out near the rear of the parking lot, a large quantity of post oak logs are stored, seasoned for eight months to exude the perfect smoky fragrance when burned.

Nina confides in me that many of Smitty's visitors are regulars. "Families come from out of town and make a day

of it," she explains. "They come with their families and when their children grow up . . . they come with their families." To satisfy their hankering, many make the trip from hundreds of miles away.

"My wife and I come out here once a month from Louisiana for brisket and sausage," brags Edgar Willows, one of the faithful who hails from Lafayette. "Sure, we got barbecue back in Louisiana, but nothing like this. Every so often we think about ribs and brisket and hop in the convertible to make the trip out here. But my wife is more crazy about the 'cue than me. She's always tellin' me that Lockhart is like the Disneyworld of barbecue."

A mere 30-minute drive south of the state capital, this quiet town of 12,000 is much more than a tourist attraction. In the

From the stairs that lead to the upper dining room at Smitty's, one can spy the pitmasters at work and get a real feel for this high temple of Texas barbecue—complete with walls and a ceiling encrusted in a heavy patina of smoke. *©2008 Coolstock/Photo by Nicole Mlakar*

spring of 1999, the Texas House of Representatives passed a resolution to recognize Lockhart as the "The Barbecue Capital of Texas." In 2003, the Texas Senate echoed the resolution, proclaiming once again that Lockhart was the Mecca of all Texas barbecue. Quite a coup for a town with only four barbecue restaurants, but not so puzzling when you learn that more than 5,000 visitors come to eat every week. In one year, roughly 250,000 people will eat barbecue in Lockhart.

Nina can sense my anticipation and can see the craving for barbecue radiating from my eyes. Without delay, she has her son and resident pitmaster John A. Fullilove prepare a sampling of meats. Fullilove is a Smitty's fixture and a local celebrity, having appeared regularly on the cover of *Texas Monthly* magazine, most recently in the article "The 50 Best Places to Eat Barbecue."

Moments later, Nina presents me with a small package that contains the meat. And this I learn is how it's done at the Texas meat market shops: the brisket, sausage, ribs, pork chops, prime rib, and any other cuts are sliced by carvers behind the counter, according to the weight that you want to buy (sort of

Driftwood, Old Fashioned Peach Cobbler

Batter
1/2 cup melted butter
1 cup flour
1 cup granulated sugar
2 teaspoons baking powder
1/4 teaspoon salt
2/3 cup room temperature milk
1 room temperature egg

Filling
1 (28-ounce) can sliced peaches, drained
(Note: best peaches to use are the O'Sage Peaches Raggedy Ripe Freestone manufactured by Margaret Holmes distributed by McCall Farms, Effingham, South Carolina)
1 cup granulated sugar
1 teaspoon cinnamon
1/2 teaspoon nutmeg

Preheat oven to 350 degrees. Melt butter in a 9x13 inch pan. In a separate bowl mix together flour, sugar, baking powder, and salt. Stir in milk and egg. Pour evenly over melted butter. In another bowl combine peaches, sugar, and spices and spread over batter—DO NOT STIR! Bake for 35–45 minutes until batter comes to the top and is golden brown.

Serve warm with ice cream

SOURCE: OLD DRIFTWOOD, TEXAS FAMILY RECIPE

like a deli counter). Just like in the old days, the meat is slapped down onto a piece of butcher paper that's pulled from a large roll. Once it's wrapped, you grab it, pay for it at the cash register, and proceed to the dining room with your precious bundle.

But the chain restaurant mentality isn't the only thing that's absent. Also coming as a surprise to those who are unfamiliar with the barbecue of this region, Smitty's doesn't serve sauce. The meat is so packed with flavor that they feel it's unnecessary. You *never* ask a man the size of his spread in Texas and at Smitty's you *never* ask "Where's the barbecue sauce?" To do so is an insult to the pitmaster. As many a pitmaster has been heard to say, "Good barbecue doesn't need sauce!"

Fortunately, the ban on sauce is as far as the culinary restrictions go. Smitty's has made concessions to customer demand and offers side-order standards like potato salad, beans, and coleslaw. Diners can also use plastic spoons and knives, but no forks. This is a throwback to the days when Texans pretty much ate meat with their bare hands, a method that is still observed at the Kreuz Market across town. Over there, they provide knives only, an homage to the days when diners sitting at the counters had to use knives that were chained to the walls.

Amid the hustle and bustle of the pitmaster juggling meats, the smell of the smoke, and the din of customers clamoring for their barbecue, I settle down at a rustic wood table in the back and dig into my samples. Both the brisket and the ribs are succulent, with just the right smokiness. The hand-made sausage is sublime. Nina explains that I'm eating what's known

Above: At Black's BBQ, the work of the pitmaster is never finished. Worrying over the meat and ensuring that the coals are always burning requires constant vigilance and patience, qualities that are reflected in the flavor of the meat. Jesse Salas tends the pit. ©2008 Coolstock/Photo by Nicole Mlakar

Left: A scene from the older meat-processing area in the rear of Smitty's Market reveals the vintage accouterments once used to run a commercial butcher shop. ©2008 Coolstock/Photo by Nicole Mlakar

as the "Central Texas–style blend," where the meat is packed loosely inside of the crinkly casings. Smitty's makes all of their own sausage right on the premises.

Over in East Texas, you are more likely to see tight, red casings packed with finely ground meat. These stubby "hot links" are a barbecue favorite throughout the state. Farther east, the town of Elgin is "The Sausage Capital of Texas" and home to the world-famous "Elgin hot guts," a hot variety of smoked sausage. Many of the barbecue restaurants that don't make their own buy their sausage in Elgin, accounting for the numerous sausage makers like Meyer's and Southside Market that form the town's central commerce.

As I digest these new barbecue factoids, I absentmindedly let a small chunk of rib meat fall to the table. When I retrieve the precious morsel, I glance at my watch and realize that I'm behind schedule. With a heavy heart, I realize that the time has come to conclude my Texas barbecue adventure and say goodbye to Nina and Smitty's. "Ya'll come back now," is what business owners always say to their customers down here, and I most definitely will.

My plan is to head north on I-35—far north, all the way through Central Texas, across the Red River, and up through Oklahoma, Kansas, and Missouri. The next region on my barbecue road trip is Kansas City, to sample the best the local legends there have to offer. My goal: one dozen barbecue joints and four regions in six days.

Junior's Creamy Coleslaw

2 cups mayonnaise
2 tablespoons cider vinegar
2 tablespoons granulated sugar
1 teaspoon minced garlic
1 teaspoon ground white pepper
1 teaspoon salt

Cabbage mix
6 large carrots peeled and shredded
1 head green cabbage, shredded

Make dressing first so it's ready to toss on vegetables as soon as they are shredded.

In a large bowl, toss the carrots and cabbage. Immediately pour dressing over cabbage. Mix and toss until all vegetables are well coated. Cover bowl and refrigerate until vegetables wilt just a little, about 15 minutes. (The flavors blend even better if slaw marinates in refrigerator about 1 hour.)

Toss again before serving to redistribute any dressing that has settled in the bottom of the bowl.

SOURCE: JUNIOR'S BARBEQUE, TEXAS, COURTESY OF THE FORT-WORTH STAR TELEGRAM, 1997

Basting the meat with "mop sauce" at Smitty's Market is a ritual performed day in and day out so that Texans making the trip to Lockhart may revel in a culinary experience like no other. ©2008 Coolstock/Photo by Nicole Mlakar

In the city of Kyle, the Railroad Bar-B-Q and Feed Store satisfies the river of traffic flowing off Interstate I-35 with their traditionally Texas barbecue menu. Here, the popular platter is the chopped or sliced brisket sandwich, along with a side order of beans and potato salad. ©2008 Michael Karl Witzel

So far, I've eaten breakfast, lunch, and dinner at three amazing barbecue shops, but my journey is far from over. In the weeks, months, and years to follow, I'll scour the Texas back roads, traverse its highways, and seek out the roads less traveled in search of more barbecue slow food. Texas is a fertile region for barbecue restaurants and it would take a special encyclopedia to cover them all.

For now, my hair and my clothing reeks of barbecue smoke and I smell like a campfire—a delicious campfire mind you—as I make one last loop around the Lockhart square and bid a fond farewell to this friendly barbecue capital. As the embers die down in the smoking pits across the German belt, the sun follows—leaving behind a barbecue dusk dappled in shades of gold and amber. In one of those rare moments that make life worth living, I look to the horizon and recall the memories I have made, the people I have met, and the flavorful barbecue I have eaten.

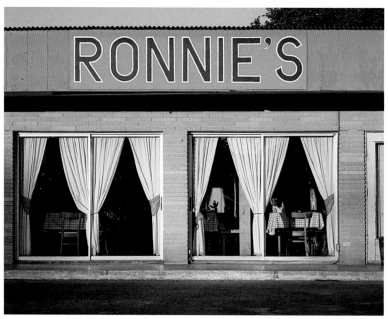

Ronnie's serves barbecue to Highway 281 travelers and the local crowd alike in Johnson City, whose namesake, Lyndon B. Johnson, was a renowned barbecue lover. Nearby, the 1960s politician held grand barbecue shindigs at the sprawling LBJ ranch. ©2008 Michael Karl Witzel

Above: America loves "Good Barbecue" and is quite fond of pork, the other white meat. In 2006 alone, the United States consumed 8.7 metric tons of it! *Author's collection*

Left: When it comes to making barbecue in the German belt of Texas, wood-fired pits and smoke are *de rigueur* for great barbecue. Not only are the pits well seasoned at Smitty's, so are the insides of the building where the open fires roar. ©2008 Coolstock/Photo by Nicole Mlakar

I come away from my Texas barbecue experience with a great sense of respect and awe for the restaurateurs, pitmasters, and barbecue shops of this region. In Driftwood, I experienced a real-life, ranch-style homestead, a Texas stereotype that sells barbecue and passes down yesterday's traditions. Farther south in old San Antonio, I had a chance to check out the best of the chain barbecue stands and learned that in Texas, excellent barbecue can sometimes be found at these franchised outfits—especially if their recipes were created by Doc Holiday. What's more, my theory that quality ingredients makes for better barbecue was confirmed at Smitty's, a Texas meat market where the quest to make a superior product leads to family loyalty.

Is everything really "bigger and better in Texas"? Possibly. What I do know for sure is that the barbecue joints in this region boast a wealth of pride, history, and technique—translating into barbecue that can truly be called legendary.

Above: Edgar and Norma Black, along with son Terry, operate Black's BBQ in Lockhart, the city officially recognized as the barbecue capital of Texas. Black's BBQ is open year-round, closing only for Thanksgiving and Christmas. ©2008 Coolstock/ Photo by Nicole Mlakar

Right: Located on East Belknap in Fort Worth, Sammie's Bar-B-Q is one of those favorite local barbecue joints that people have been going to for years. Established in 1946, it has turned out smoked delights for decades, relying on four wood-fired pits to cook up barbecue staples such as beef, ribs, chicken, ham, and turkey. ©2008 Michael Karl Witzel

In Lockhart, Black's lays claim to being the oldest barbecue restaurant in the state of Texas continuously run by the same family. But for many, it's the good food and no-frills atmosphere that brings them in to dine. ©2008 Coolstock/Photo by Nicole Mlakar

Above: In Hamilton, the Smoke Shack Pit Bar-B-Q battles it out with a Dairy Queen to the south and a Chicken Express to the north. It's not much of a fight, since the residents of this region hold their barbecue dear. ©2008 Michael Karl Witzel

Right: In Texas, barbecue stands are virtually everywhere. This Pappas Bar-B-Q outpost is doing a respectable business right inside of the Houston Airport, greeting new arrivals with one of the state's most popular combos: slow-smoked barbecue and beer. ©2008 Michael Karl Witzel

Crazy about Coleslaw

Coleslaw got its name from the Dutch *koolsalade* or "cabbage salad" during the eighteenth century. In the Netherlands, native speakers often shortened the term to *koolsla*, which English visitors picked up as "coleslaw." In England, the dish was referred to as "cold" slaw until the 1860s when "cole," originating from the Latin *colis* or "cabbage," returned to use.

By the 1900s, coleslaw had landed on America's shores. Its popularity surged in 1912 after New York City deli owner Richard Hellmann began marketing premade mayonnaise. His wife's tasty recipe became so popular that Hellmann began selling it in "wooden boats" that were used for weighing butter. Hellmann's Blue Ribbon Mayonnaise was a bona fide time saver for the American housewife.

Because cooking with mayonnaise was now as easy as opening a jar, and cabbage was an affordable staple, adding coleslaw to the repertoire of dinnertime side dishes was a no-brainer. Its sublime blend of crisp, shredded cabbage and savory spices made the Dutch-inspired salad the perfect accompaniment for no-nonsense entrées like burgers, fried chicken, sandwiches, and barbecue.

Barbecue is where the side dish literally became part of the main dish itself. As far back as any pitmaster can recall, traditional Memphis- and Carolina-style pulled-pork sandwiches have been crowned with coleslaw. That means on top of the meat and under the bun—providing a tasty medley of bread, barbecue sauce, pork, and slaw in every bite.

But not every barbecue region has adopted coleslaw as an integral part of its sandwich architecture. In the Lone Star State—where sliced (and chopped) beef brisket dominates the pits—it's not unusual to hear someone utter "Get a rope!" when they witness an epicure from out of town top their sliced brisket sandwich with a scooped lump of slaw.

In Kansas City, the gourmands of barbecue are a little more forgiving. Although fans of this region typically do not use coleslaw as a condiment, they are likely to turn a blind eye to those who display a penchant for topping their pulled-pig sandwiches with the shredded cabbage mix.

Some cooks—like those at Leonard's Pit Barbecue in Memphis—add dry mustard to create a spicy, zesty slaw. Meanwhile, cooks in Lexington, North Carolina, include ingredients such as ketchup and Texas Pete brand hot sauce to create their red slaw, a much-loved part of what the BBQ cognoscenti refer to as the "Lexington Barbecue Sandwich."

Ultimately, the regional differences in coleslaw are only variations on a theme. Throughout the four barbecue regions and beyond, it's a dining essential. As long as it's crisp, rich with flavor, and not runny, coleslaw will remain synonymous with pulled, chopped, or sliced pork sandwiches—whether dressed with oil and vinegar, mayonnaise, or something completely different.

Southern-style mustard coleslaw. Parker's Barbecue, Wilson, North Carolina.
©2008 Michael Karl Witzel

Kreuz Market

619 North Colorado Street
Lockhart, Texas 78644
(512) 398-2361

It's 10:30 on a Saturday morning and already the line at Kreuz is snaking its way out into the parking lot. A sign at the front entrance alerts the novice to the rules of the house:

No Barbecue Sauce (Nothing To Hide)
No Forks (They Are At the End of Your Arm)
No Salads (Remember No Forks)
No Credit (Cards Also) (Bank Doesn't Sell Barbecue)
No Kidding (See Owner's Face)

When you enter the door, the first thing that greets your nostrils is a distinct aroma of wood smoke—mingled with the heavenly scent of meat. In line, some folks strike up pleasant conversations with their neighbors. Others fix their gaze toward their ultimate goal: the meat counter.

It's a mixed bag of customers, from the cowboy wearing faded Wranglers, to the tourist clad in a loud Hawaiian shirt, to the local youth decked out in an "I Ate It All!" T-shirt. All have one thing in common: a love for some of the best barbecue that Texas has to offer. Some live around the corner, but most have traveled over 60 miles just to nibble on tender Kreuz brisket.

In the true Texas tradition of mixing politics with barbecue, one man stands out above the rest, wearing a placard that reads "Kinky Friedman for Governor." Alas, poor Kinky (and yes, that is his real name) did not win the gubernatorial. Kinky, a regular writer for *Texas Monthly* magazine, musician, and all-around Texas character, was doing what Texas politicians have been doing best since the inception of Texas politics: mixing some steer with a little bull and spicing it up with a heaping serving of smiles. You can't get more Texan than that!

Kreuz Market is Texas big, bright, and bountiful. With easy access to and from the freeway, its prime location accounts for the large percentage of customers who stream through its doors daily. When Rick Schmidt first built this place in 1999, the idea was to accommodate customers by maximizing work flow and providing room for growth. He succeeded, and today the well-lit eatery has a seating capacity of 570, with room for an additional 240 on the front porch. The four service counters keep a steady line of customers moving forward, preventing any bottlenecks.

The heart and heat of Kreuz is in its pits—long brick chutes with open fires at one end and counterweighted metal lids on top. Their design dates back hundreds of years, a simple system that gets the job done. As Rick's son Keith Schmidt explains, "The design is basically a crude convection oven in that you have fire and indirect heat at one end and a chimney at the other end, which causes a natural draw so you are pulling smoke and heat, rushing across the meat. Throughout the length of the pit, you have cool and hot spots, so you move the meat to wherever you need it. If you need more heat, you move it up to the front or close to back. For less heat, we move it to the middle."

Manning one of the cutting blocks is Roy Perez, a Kreuz 20-year veteran. Sporting Elvis sideburns, he wields his knife with finesse, slicing up some of the best 'cue your taste buds will ever experience.

(continued overleaf)

Kreuz Market is a relatively new building in Lockhart, Texas, built solely for hosting the large crowds that make their way to this town every day for barbecue. The original Kreuz Market began in the downtown square, in the space now occupied by Smitty's Market. ©2008 Coolstock/Photo by Nicole Mlakar

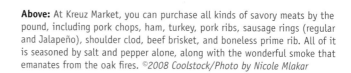

Above: At Kreuz Market, you can purchase all kinds of savory meats by the pound, including pork chops, ham, turkey, pork ribs, sausage rings (regular and Jalapeño), shoulder clod, beef brisket, and boneless prime rib. All of it is seasoned by salt and pepper alone, along with the wonderful smoke that emanates from the oak fires. ©2008 Coolstock/Photo by Nicole Mlakar

Left: As the lunchtime crowds ebb, Kreuz Market pit cook Pete Castillo rests momentarily and contemplates the morning's events. His day is filled with nonstop activity—tending to the pits, making sure that the fires are burning, and that ample meat is loaded. ©2008 Coolstock/Photo by Nicole Mlakar

On butcher paper, he stacks up tender slices of prime rib, brisket, a ring of Kreuz sausage, pork chops, and some ribs. The order is handed off to Ella Townes, another Kreuz veteran who is over 70 years young. Then, the meat is weighed, a total given, and the customer hands over the greenbacks.

One thing is for sure: the customers who know a good thing keep coming back. It's no wonder. The Kreuz tradition goes all the way back to the year 1900 when Charles Kreuz opened up his butcher shop and grocery on the square in Lockhart, Texas. Kreuz installed an outdoor barbecue pit behind the store and began smoking meat. In those days, there was no refrigeration, so smoking was a good way to prevent spoilage.

From the start, Kreuz offered a no-frills method of serving defined by butcher paper and no cutlery. Regardless, the smoked delight was a hit with the field hands, who worked up quite an appetite planting and harvesting Lockhart's cash crop: cotton.

In 1935, 15-year-old Edgar Schmidt went to work for the Kreuz family. By 1948, he owned the business but kept the Kreuz name on the operation. At the time, it was still primarily a meat market—with pits in the back and sausage-making going at full tilt—orchestrated by a man known as Houston "Dummy" Wright. Edgar Schmidt's three children, Rick, Don, and Nina grew up amid the pits, the sausage-making, and the ever-constant smoke.

Top left: For those unfamiliar with Texas barbecue, it's difficult to fathom the sheer number of pits that Kreuz Market uses to prepare its product. Without a doubt, this is a Texas-sized operation, catering to the Texas-sized appetite for barbecue that keeps the town of Lockhart humming. **Top right:** Inside Kreuz Market, a long line of customers awaits their turn to place their meat order. Once the barbecue is secured, there is another area and another line where customers order side dishes and soft drinks. If you're hungry, have one family member wait in each line and make plans to meet at a predetermined table! **Bottom right:** Inside the cavernous interior of Kreuz Market, diners can choose from a number of areas to sit and eat their meat: a cozy, air-conditioned space near the side order line, a quieter space near the center of the building, or even an enclosed patio area with open-air screens and long wooden tables to catch the overflow crowds.
Bottom left: Assistant manager and pitmaster Roy Perez takes his carving duties seriously. His years of experience at Kreuz Market afford him the skill to gauge visually exactly how much he is slicing off. Who needs a scale? *All ©2008 Coolstock/Photo by Nicole Mlakar*

In 1984, Edgar was ready to retire. So, his two sons, Don and Rick, purchased the equipment, goodwill, and the rights to the Kreuz name from their father. They formed their own corporation and named it Kreuz Sausage & Barbecue Company, Inc. Don retired in 1996 and Rick went ahead and moved the whole operation to its new and present location, opening to the public on September 1, 1999. Now, a third generation has stepped in to continue this Texas tradition: Keith Schmidt, who got involved in 1997.

During all of these changes, the family has remained true to its origins and maintained one constant: the art of sausage-making. Steeped in the state's German culture, sausage has been and always will be a staple at the pits of South Texas. To this day, the original recipe perfected and standardized by Rick Schmidt is still used to make the succulent rings.

Keith explains, "Back then there was no recipe. It was kind of whatever was around. My father actually put a recipe down to it in 1982 or 1983. We use 85 percent beef and 15 percent pork with varying degrees of fat. Salt, pepper, and cayenne are the spices. It's real simple. The flavor is not muddied up with a lot of different spices." Indeed,

the award-winning Kreuz sausage rings are big on flavor, with just the right amount of smoke.

But if you don't live close enough to Lockhart to make the drive, don't despair. Nowadays, you can have your sausage sent to you. In 2004, Kreuz received USDA certification and now ships their flavorful rings of meat to all 50 states.

They also wholesale it to restaurants. In fact, one of their latest customers is Hill Country New York, a New York restaurant owned by a friend of Keith's. A direct takeoff of the Kreuz barbecue operation, they conduct business with one exception: They do accept credit cards!

CHAPTER 2

Kansas City

BRAGGING OF BARBECUE BIG AND BOLD

"KANSAS CITY, HERE I COME!" It may sound cliché, but it's the one lyric that rings true in my mind as I drive north on Interstate 35 through Texas, Oklahoma, and Kansas. As the song says, they have "some crazy little women there," but my mission is to meet up with another mistress: that smoky, smoldering temptress called barbecue.

In this case, I'm not taking a bus, riding on a train, or flying in a plane. I'm not walking, either. On this leg of my trip to discover the second region of legendary American barbecue, I'm rockin' down the highway on two wheels, straddling a two-tone, cream- and turquoise-flamed Harley-Davidson Fatboy. I'm riding straight into the heart of Kansas City, Missouri, a place that bills itself as "The Barbecue Capital of the World," bound for the area that Wilbert Harrison sang about in his 1959 hit: 18th Street and Vine, the cradle of Kansas City 'cue.

During the 1920s, Kansas City's 12th Street became nationally known for its profusion of nightclubs, gambling parlors, and brothels—earning the city the moniker, "The Paris of the Plains." At its zenith, 12th Street was a hot spot, with more than 50 jazz clubs. Just six blocks to the north at 18th and Vine, jazz also flourished and helped to bring national attention to what many regarded as the epicenter of the African-American community.

Above: Arthur Bryant's isn't big on potato salad. Here, the homemade French fries get all the attention. Of course, they are made from real potatoes (with the skins) and are never frozen. On a typical day, huge plastic tubs full of them await their turn to be fried as customers make orders. *©2008 Michael Karl Witzel*

Right: Located on 60th and Troost in Kansas City, Blue Hills Barbecue was one of the many restaurants that helped to establish the barbecue traditions of the region. *Author's collection*

Opposite: *People* magazine once reported that "Arthur Bryant's has long been to barbecue what the statue of liberty was to immigration. . . . The place is a beacon to all barbecue lovers." With platters of food looking this amazing, it's easy to see why. *©2008 Michael Karl Witzel*

New Deal–style public works projects that kept the residents employed and fed the political machine needed to keep the dance-oriented nightlife swinging. During the 1920s through the late 1930s, jazz musicians from all points migrated here in search of jobs and to find a receptive audience for their talents.

But there was much more to the Kansas City African-American community than the jazz music scene. Many who migrated to the area became successful entrepreneurs as well. They opened barbershops, pressing houses, publishing concerns, drugstores, and other businesses. The economic expansion also provided a favorable climate for restaurants, particularly no-frills greasy spoons that served up moist and tasty barbecue.

Up from this verdant garden of prosperity rose a man by the name of Henry Perry, cited by barbecue historians as the progenitor of Kansas City barbecue himself. At the turn of the twentieth century he came to town from Shelby County, Tennessee, near Memphis, and brought with him the skills needed to turn pork ribs into profit.

Perry began to serve his barbecue to Kansas Citians in 1907. His first eatery was a small hole-in-the-wall stand on a Banks Street alley, which he later relocated to a rehabilitated streetcar on 19th and Highland, in the African-American neighborhood around 18th Street and Vine. His bill of fare was limited, but well received. For 25 cents, the hungry horn player, cabbie, or businessman could dine on a slab of slow-cooked ribs, wrapped in newsprint.

But Perry's stand was only the beginning of Kansas City barbecue. Blessed with the meeting of the Kansas and Missouri rivers and the joining of major railroads, the city was a shipping hub for the livestock industry. Meatpackers like Armour Brothers and Swift Company (which had a four-story smoking house) headquartered there. From the 1860s to the 1960s, processing cured meats and shipping them nationwide was the second largest industry in the world.

Above the interior facade inside the Emanuel Cleaver location of Gates Bar-B-Q, artisans have re-created the advertisements that once adorned the exterior of the Ol' Kentuck Bar-B-Q on 19th and Vine in Kansas City. *©2008 Michael Karl Witzel*

By the 1930s, Kansas City had no equal when it came to entertainment. Under the reign of politico "Boss Tom" Pendergast and his cronies, white lightning and wine flowed freely during the Prohibition years and the good times rolled. With its frontier mentality, the town was "wide-open." Mobsters claimed their turf and bootlegging became a growth industry, dwarfed only by the burgeoning meatpacking industry.

At the same time, Kansas City was insulated from the worst effects of the Great Depression, due in large part to

Left: Arthur Bryant, the legendary "King of Ribs," is the most renowned barbecuer in history. He created a spicy, thick, and rich Kansas City–style sauce that has attracted the likes of former presidents Harry Truman and Jimmy Carter to his restaurant, considered the best in the world by *The New Yorker* columnist Calvin Trillin. ©2008 *Michael Karl Witzel*

Below: Some say Charlie Bryant started the Kansas City barbecue tradition. Others say it was Henry Perry, for whom Charlie worked. Arthur visited his brother Charlie in Kansas City and never left. Charlie owned the business after Henry died, and after Charlie died, Arthur took over. Arthur first perfected Perry's original sauce by adding molasses ("I make it so you can put it on bread and eat it") and then opened the 18th and Brooklyn restaurant that was to become a legend. ©2008 *Michael Karl Witzel*

A sliced ham sandwich is painted with a hefty dollop of Arthur Bryant's signature sauce and cradled between two slices of white bread. Beautiful. Another edible masterpiece is ready to serve—and eat. ©2008 Michael Karl Witzel

Charles Perry readies the ingredients for another barbecue sandwich as customers line up for their food on the other side of the pass-through windows. During lunch, Arthur Bryant's kitchen is a nonstop frenzy of slicing, sandwich-making, and sauce-slathering. ©2008 Michael Karl Witzel

The original Brooklyn Avenue Arthur Bryant's location is managed by 'cue man Eddie Echols (behind the register). Here, the most serious of all Kansas City transactions takes place: the exchange of legal tender for another kind of tender: barbecued meat. ©2008 Michael Karl Witzel

With the widespread availability of beef and pork, butchers were busy, as was the growing rabble of "grease houses," a nickname given to the barbecue joints of the region. The glut of meat resulted in low prices for everyone and made the so-called "lower quality" cuts an out-and-out bargain. Seeing opportunity in the bonanza, African-American cooks who already knew how to transform the ordinary into the extraordinary "got busy with it" and created the Kansas City barbecue legend, one smoked rib at a time.

As word of the town's barbecue largess got out, the barbecue business in "The Heart of America" put down roots and began to grow. By 1932, Kansas City's leading black newspaper, *The Call*, noted that "more than a thousand barbecue stands" were doing business in town.

Above: Since 1930, celebrities such as Steven Spielberg, Michael Landon, Robert Redford, Jack Nicholson, Wilt Chamberlain, Bryant Gumbel, Tom Watson, and George Brett—as well as common folk—have made the pilgrimage to Arthur Bryant's to enjoy barbecue that's slow-smoked with a combination of hickory and oak woods, mellowed to the peak of flavor, then splashed with Arthur Bryant's Original or Rich & Spicy sauce. ©2008 Michael Karl Witzel

Left: In Kansas City, Arthur Bryant's still uses the real pit-smoking method for preparing their barbecue. Hickory logs are added to a firebox, from which the smoke and heat are drawn into the cooking chamber where the meat resides. ©2008 Michael Karl Witzel

Kansas City Sloppy Ribs

1 cup packed brown sugar
1/2 cup paprika
2-1/2 tablespoons ground black pepper
2-1/2 tablespoons salt
1-1/2 tablespoons chili powder
1-1/2 tablespoons garlic powder
1-1/2 tablespoons onion powder
1 teaspoon ground cayenne pepper
3 full slabs of pork spareribs "St. Louis cut" (trimmed off the chine bone and brisket flap) preferably 3 pounds each or less
Sweet tomato-based barbecue sauce

The night before you plan to barbecue, combine brown sugar, paprika, black pepper, salt, chili powder, garlic powder, onion powder and red pepper. Apply about a third of the spice mixture evenly to ribs, reserving remainder. Place ribs in a plastic bag; refrigerate overnight. Before you begin to barbecue, sprinkle ribs lightly but thoroughly with spice mixture, reserving remainder. Let ribs sit at room temperature for 30–40 minutes.

Prepare smoker, bringing the temperature to 200–220 degrees. Transfer ribs to smoker. Cook about 4 hours, turning and sprinkling ribs with spice mixture after about 2 hours. In the last 45 minutes of cooking, slather ribs once or twice with barbecue sauce.

When ready, the meat will bend easily between the ribs, and the sauce will be gooey and sticky. Allow slabs to sit for 10 minutes before slicing them into individual ribs. Serve with more sauce on top or on the side and plenty of napkins.

Yield: 6 servings

SOURCE: ADAPTED FROM "SMOKE AND SPICE." ©1998 PHILADELPHIA NEWSPAPERS INC.

The devotees of Arthur Bryant's barbecue are unlike any other. According to reports, some have even sent private jets to pick up sandwiches piled high with smoky ham or beef, along with mounds of French fries. Here, you can choose from three types of thick, Kansas City–style sauces (made with tomatoes, sugar, vinegar, and other secret ingredients): Original, Rich & Spicy, and Sweet Heat. ©2008 Michael Karl Witzel

Indeed, Perry was "The Barbecue King" of Kansas City, and under his tutelage a long list of ascendants to his throne learned the craft from the old master. Among the hopefuls were Charlie and Arthur Bryant, who were involved with the now-legendary barbecue shop known as Arthur Bryant's, the joint that author Calvin Trillin described as the "best damn restaurant in the world" in a 1974 article for *The New Yorker* magazine.

A man by the name of Arthur Pinkard also served under Perry and later emerged as a skilled pitmaster in his own right.

A loner, often referred to by historians as the "mystery man," he worked the pits at a 19th and Vine restaurant called the Ol' Kentuck Bar-B-Q, an eatery owned by Johnny Thomas that sold barbecue and bootleg whiskey.

GATES BAR-B-Q, EMANUEL CLEAVER BOULEVARD

In 1946, Mr. George Gates strutted onto the Kansas City barbecue stage and bought the Ol' Kentuck Bar-B-Q, weary of the racial tension he had experienced in his previous jobs. Gates was a railroad steward when race dictated that he shouldn't be one, and later the first African-American postal clerk in town. As the story goes, when his boss told him that "he had a white man's job," he said "then give it to him" and quit. Barbecue became his destiny.

To get the rest of the story, I'm visiting the Gates Bar-B-Q restaurant that's become a Kansas City landmark over on Emanuel Cleaver Boulevard, one of six locations in town run by members of the Gates family. The current flagship restaurant

Ollie Gates' Barbecue Sauce Recipe

This recipe is a close approximation to the famous Ollie Gates recipe. It was featured on an episode of "From Martha's Kitchen" on the Food Network about five years ago.

1 cup sugar
1/4 cup salt
2 tablespoons celery seed
2 tablespoons ground cumin
2 tablespoons ground cayenne pepper
2 tablespoons garlic powder
1 tablespoon chili powder
2 quarts ketchup
2 cups apple cider vinegar
1-1/2 teaspoons liquid smoke
1 teaspoon freshly squeezed lemon juice

In a small bowl, combine sugar, salt, celery seed, cumin, red pepper, garlic powder, and chili powder. Set aside.

In a large bowl, combine ketchup, vinegar, liquid smoke, and lemon juice. Add dry ingredients and mix until very well blended. Serve warm or at room temperature.

Sauce may be stored in an airtight container in refrigerator for up to 3 weeks or in freezer for up to 6 months.

Yield: about 3 quarts

SOURCE: COURTESY OF GATES BAR-B-Q, KANSAS CITY, MISSOURI

Struttin' with Gates is what barbecue is all about in Kansas City. With multiple locations around town, the Gates family can indeed walk proud, knowing that their barbecue traditions continue to shape this town's restaurant business. *©2008 Michael Karl Witzel*

Right: Gates Bar-B-Q began at the Ol' Kentuck, located at the bustling nexus of early Kansas City African-American culture, 19th Street and Vine, seen here circa 1948. *Courtesy of Ollie Gates*

Below: At Gates, the sight of a full rack of ribs staggers the imagination. Along with a bottle of soda pop, potato salad, and plate of bread, there is barely enough room left on the serving tray for barbecue sauce. *©2008 Michael Karl Witzel*

Ollie Gates' Barbecue Beans

2 cans baked beans
1/2 cup firmly packed dark brown sugar
1/2 cup molasses
3 tablespoons rib seasoning (recipe on opposite page)
3/4 cup barbecue sauce (recipe on page 60)
1 teaspoon liquid smoke

In a cast-iron pot, combine beans, brown sugar, molasses, rib seasoning, barbecue sauce, and liquid smoke. Cook on the grill, stirring occasionally, until hardened "crust" forms on top of beans (approximately 20 minutes).

SOURCE: COURTESY OF GATES BAR-B-Q, KANSAS CITY, MISSOURI

Inside the Emanuel Cleaver location, Gates Bar-B-Q features a re-creation of the 19th and Vine Street scene where the first restaurant was located. All of the details of the Ol' Kentuck are here, including street lamps, signs, and more.
©2008 Michael Karl Witzel

fired up its pits in 2000 and has been stopping traffic ever since. On the lush green lawn out in front, a 20-foot statue of the whimsical Gates "Struttin' Man" stands sentinel over traffic.

Upon entering the building, it's as if you stepped back in time. A re-creation of an old-time trolley car greets you on the left, where you get in line to make your order. Over to the right, the Gates family has replicated the street facade of 19th and Vine as it looked during the heyday of the Ol' Kentuck. Along with white stonework and hand-lettered window signs, they have even included the upper story window where a lady used to call down the locations of new fares to the cab drivers who queued up below on the street.

Ollie Gates, the son of founder George Gates, tells me of a legend that is still very much in the making. He starts by describing a much different time and place in Kansas City. Like a movie narrator, he relates the happy and bittersweet moments that formed the brickwork of the Gates legacy.

During those early days when his dad was first getting the Ol' Kentuck going, he recalls how his mother Arzelia had to rein in his father when it came to what sort of products they would sell there. Apparently, Arzelia had a higher moral standard and decided that there was no way they were going to sell barbecue from a would-be speakeasy.

"My mother's role was to keep everything on the level," Ollie explains. "She said to my dad, 'You've gotta stop doing some of things you are doing in the basement and clean the act up and turn it into a wholesome restaurant.' My mother was a very religious lady. She wanted to make sure that my father—and everyone else there—stayed on the right track."

Fortunately, they were already on the right track when it came to the cooking, as Mr. Arthur Pinkard came along with the deal. "Mr. Arthur had a unique way about him because he always used a little pinch of this and a little pinch of that," recalls Ollie. "My father learned to weigh those little pinches and that is how he came up with the formulas we use today. From him, my father learned all about the nature of different spices and how they reacted with certain foods."

In 1951, a fire destroyed the 19th and Vine location and George Gates moved to 24th and Brooklyn. Despite the move, the nature of the business didn't change much. "When I left in

1949 to go to college, the business wasn't like the business you see today," Ollie explains. "Back then, it was a smoke-filled joint that had no air-conditioning, no exhaust fans, and it worked you all day—and all night—every day." For these reasons and more, Ollie never imagined that he would ever seriously pursue a career in barbecue.

But life had other plans, and eventually experience softened his hard attitude toward the family business. "After a few years of experience with college and then the army—seven years to be exact—I came back and I saw things in a different light," he confesses. "All of a sudden, I could see the endless possibilities of this barbecue business and that it could be a lot more than just a 'shack by the track.' We had some opportunities that were presenting themselves and so I decided that I wanted to pursue some of them."

And that's how Ollie officially entered (for the second time) the barbecue business. When he got out of the army, he opened a new Gates location at 12th and Brooklyn, but it didn't take long before his father booted him out of the nest. "Now it's time to go build your own," his father said, setting Ollie on the path to meet his destiny. "When my dad and I were together it was called Gates and Son," recalls Ollie, letting out a brief chuckle. "But every time he'd get mad at me, he'd take off the 'and Son' part."

Like any son, Ollie had his own ideas and wanted to do things differently than his dad. The first part of his plan was to clean up the image of the barbecue joint. "Back then, barbecue wasn't at all acceptable for people who went out to fancy nightclubs in their formal attire, doing things that were 'high-end,'" he explains. "I wanted to let everybody know that barbecue was just as appropriate for the society guy wearing a top hat and tails as it was for the working man right off the street in overalls. Either way, you could be just as proud to strut in the door. And that's what strutting with Gates barbecue is all about."

The second part of Ollie's plan was to improve the quality of the food and how it was prepared. "When we first began, the theme of the barbecue industry was defined by the most awful forms of cooking: outdoors, in the backyard, using cheap meats, the poor end of the animal—whether it was a pig or a cow, it made no difference," he explains. "We decided to use a better grade of meat, and as a result made barbecue

Ollie Gates' Rib Rub

1 cup sugar
1/2 cup salt
2 tablespoons paprika
2 tablespoons red pepper
1 tablespoon cumin
1 tablespoon ground celery

Mix together and store in container.

SOURCE: COURTESY OF GATES BAR-B-Q, KANSAS CITY, MISSOURI

A prep cook hacks up some Gates sausage, preparing one of the many barbecue combination platters that the restaurant serves. ©2008 Michael Karl Witzel

SANDWICHES

CHICKEN	30¢
TENDERLOIN	15¢
FISH	15¢
BRAIN	15¢
HAMBURGER	15¢
SNOUT	15¢
EARS	10¢
HOT DOG	10

more acceptable." Ollie also instituted cafeteria-style service so the average Joe could buy that better cut at a fair price, feel comfortable, and not have to worry about tips.

But rehabilitating the reputation and quality of barbecue was only the beginning for Ollie Gates. During his stint in the army, he attended basic training at the engineering school at Fort Belvoir, Virginia. Later—when combined with his studies from Lincoln University—he found that he had a much deeper well to draw upon for improving his tarnished trade. "My army training provided me with the regimented perspective needed to better organize my restaurant," he says. "And my years at Lincoln gave me the skills I needed to build."

Unfortunately, Ollie's father wasn't so keen on all of the changes that he wanted to make in the early Gates joints, some of which involved taking a closer look at the inventory to see if any profits were being made. Like the prophet who was not respected in his hometown, Ollie didn't get the props he deserved. He recalls wistfully, "I tried to make some sense of the place, but my dad was working there and he took exception to what I was doing to the business—his business." Ironically, his father passed away before he could witness how effective many of Ollie's great ideas were.

Later, when he managed his very own barbecue joint, Ollie got downright scientific with his logical approach. To better track what was coming in and what was going out, he applied the tenets of inventory analysis that he learned in the military and introduced daily report sheets and logs. When he applied the plans in earnest, the process proved viable. It allowed him to compete on the same playing field with the fast food stands that were already doing business in such a regimented manner.

Ollie's voice gets serious when he states, "We cleaned it up, we packaged it right, and we also made all the packaging

Gates pitmaster Brian Channel retrieves one of the many racks of ribs cooking in the restaurant's wood-fired ovens. Controlled by dampers, the ovens require an experienced hand who knows how to cook by look and feel, not by timers and temperature. ©2008 Michael Karl Witzel

Gates Bar-B-Q manufactures its own line of barbecue sauces that are sold in local stores and by mail order. In Kansas City, barbecue and sauce go in hand. Sure, there's a lot to be said for tasting the meat, but when the barbecue sauce is this good, who can resist the combination? ©2008 Michael Karl Witzel

for the product to go in. We packaged it all in a neat-looking outfit. We cleaned up the restaurant—the outside and the inside—and added a little bit of style to it. We came up with some nice verbiage and an attractive look. All those things became part of the package. When people came to accept that product—the way we presented it and the way it tasted—the more people jumped on board with Gates."

Those people—regular customers and new ones—were important, and Ollie was wise enough to realize it. Having good food and a nice place was all well and good, but it was customers who made the business. So Ollie adopted the now familiar greeting, "Hi, may I help you?" and instructed his help to use it whenever a new customer came in. "It's just a part of what we call our initial 'counter conversation'," says

Beer started the whole Rosedale Bar-B-Q legacy way back in 1934. Its precursor, appropriately named The Bucket Shop, specialized in selling beer by the bucket-load at a quarter apiece. "You bring the bucket and we'll fill it," was their sales motto. ©2008 Michael Karl Witzel

Ollie. Today, the greeting is reproduced in glowing neon up on the wall at the Emanuel Cleaver store.

Sensing an opening, I ask if I might be able to take advantage of that well-known service and have a quick taste. While my samples are being prepared, pitmaster Brian Channel gives me a close-up look at the pits—and a show—as he opens one of the doors to retrieve a beautiful hunk of meat. With its glossy walls built with bright-red bricks, this kitchen looks exactly like a barbecue kitchen ought to look.

For fuel, Gates Bar-B-Q uses real oak and hickory. "Inside, our pits are 4 feet by 8 feet deep and 6 feet long," says Ollie. "There are two or three different levels, so there are two to three different temperatures." It's a tricky, hands-on process, learned through years of hard work. Ollie explains, "We run it by dampers that we close off, to allow it to have more smoke in one spot and less in another. We do it by dampers and by feel rather than by timers and temperature. Feel and touch, that's what makes it an art."

Behind the scenes, kitchen helpers are busy preparing meat and sides for the growing list of orders in the service area. Carefully, they slice up sausage, arrange ribs, and position slabs of brisket on large trays (they call their biggest the "President's

Hayward's Pit Bar B Que boasts 7,000 square feet of dining space with 222 available seats. The barbecue sauce and rub are made right there on the premises and shipped everywhere in the country. ©2008 Michael Karl Witzel

Choice" tray). It's much too busy for me to sit down and eat right now, so I'm served small samples of select menu items and consume them as we move about, touring the kitchen.

Things are picking up now and it's getting busy, so I move out of the way and head for the customer area. At the front counter, overlapping greetings of "Hi, may I help you?" are heard as people patiently wait their turn in line. The little trolley is full of customers now and the dining rooms on the re-created 18th and Vine Street side are filled with barbecue lovers. If you relax, you can almost imagine what it must have been like during those hazy, crazy days of barbecue.

"So this is what Kansas City barbecue is all about," I say, pointing to the beehive of activity. "Yes, it's a way of life," replies Ollie. "That's what you have to understand. When we first started, the industry wasn't as clean and pretty as it is now. I helped clean it up and make it acceptable. You lived the business to make sure that it did what you wanted it to. I call it a marriage. Today it's a way of life, and now I can't break away."

Unfortunately, it's time for me to break away. I give Ollie my sincere thanks for the great food and for a glimpse into the city's history. Like the Gates struttin' man, I swagger smartly toward the exit and amble out the door, happy in the fact that I've had the chance to get the lowdown on the Gates family and their dynasty of Kansas City barbecue restaurants.

HAYWARD'S PIT BAR B QUE, ANTIOCH BOULEVARD Although Gates Bar-B-Q is a major link in the history of Kansas City barbecue restaurants, numerous other eateries in town are striving to attain the rank of legend. One such restaurant is Hayward's Pit Bar B Que, an up-and-coming joint filling the air with the sweet smell of barbecue smoke out on Antioch Boulevard, just south of downtown. It's run by a magnificent gent by the name of Hayward Spears, a self-made pit man who opened the place during the 1970s when Kansas City 'cue was picking up steam.

I pull into Hayward's parking lot and notice an odd coincidence: the building's red bricks look like those that were used to build the meatpacking warehouses that once loomed over this toddling town. Inside, dressed in coal-black slacks and matching shirt, a modest display of gold chains hinting at his success, owner Hayward Spears shakes my hand and welcomes me.

The Hayward Spears story echoes the work ethic of the early African-American pioneers who made the city's barbecue what

Hayward's pits are rotisserie-style units. Inside, a Ferris wheel type of rack holds the meat, providing more even heat and less labor. In a flat brick pit, the meat must be constantly moved by hand. ©2008 Michael Karl Witzel

it is today. "I came to Kansas City 53 years ago," he begins, a sense of seriousness shaping his demeanor. "My father was a businessman, an entrepreneur, the first black man to buy his own farm in Arkansas in the early 1940s, before World War II broke out. Unlike most Afro-American sharecroppers back then, my dad owned his own farm and he believed in everybody owning their own business."

Growing up in that atmosphere, Spears was destined to go into business for himself and tried his hand at a number

"We make our own rub seasoning that we put on the product," says Hayward Spears, owner of Hayward's Pit Bar B Que. "The rub is applied directly to the meat and then it sits overnight." ©2008 Michael Karl Witzel

of occupations, first as the owner of janitorial service and then later, as a factory worker at the General Motors plant. On nights, weekends, and holidays, he devoted his time to perfecting his barbecue artistry. Over the years, he developed such a love for the form that in 1972 he decided to hang out his own shingle and open a restaurant.

The preparation area at Hayward's Pit Bar B Que is arranged for speed and simplicity. When the meat is removed from the pits, it goes directly to the slicing table, where it is quickly prepared by Pedro Galvan Lopez and served to the customers, piping hot. ©2008 Michael Karl Witzel

"My barbecue didn't start out as a business, but as a hobby," he explains. "When my coworkers at General Motors would go to play at the golf course, I went into my backyard and worked at cooking up some barbecue. Well, the word eventually got around town that I was fixing some really *good* barbecue, so I started making it for civic and political groups and anybody else that I could entice to try it."

Spears was serious about his hobby and built three barbecue pits in his backyard when he was first honing his technique. "I'm a workaholic and like to create things from nothing," he states. Today, the large pits in his restaurant are similar in design to the ones he used at home. Of course, these cookers, built by a Texas firm called Oyler, are outfitted with rotisseries and all of the other bells and whistles one might need in a restaurant.

The tandem steel-enclosed pits are built into a heavy brick wall, accented by an arched course of bricks above, lending a certain industrial flair to the cooking area of the kitchen. At the center of the two smokers, a heavy wrought-iron gate with

cast filigree guards the service alley and echoes the brickwork with a fanciful arch of its own. Set into a heavy plate of steel painted gloss black, the words "Hayward's Pit" are engraved in gold relief.

Hayward's ovens are "one-of-a-kind," a phrase that Spears fancies should describe barbecue in general. With a look of knowing, he doesn't mind telling me that "One of the principal reasons why nobody has been very successful in franchising barbecue is because in order for barbecue to be good and at its very best—the way it was meant to be—it has to be prepared

At Hayward's Pit Bar B Que, ribs are the specialty. "It goes right back to my dad and growing up," explains Spears. "The pork spareribs are our signature item. Even though it is beef country, all the barbecue houses in Kansas City have pork spareribs. ©2008 Michael Karl Witzel

directly on the premises where it is being served." Old school all the way, Spears is not impressed by mail-order barbecue.

He lifts his hand in the direction of his pit and the racks of ribs that are being taken out by one of his cooks and says, "You can't have a commissary in Kansas City and another outlet in Los Angeles and have it shipped there. The food will lose all its flavor and texture while in transport. I think that's what sets barbecue apart from other food products, the frozen fast food hamburgers."

I take him up on the challenge, find a table, and fix my iced tea with squeezed lemon and sugar as I wait to be served a plate of his specialty: pork ribs. Kansas City is all about beef, but pork still manages to find its way into the barbecue joints of this region. After a few hearty bites, I agree with his theory and slather on some of his signature sauce, hot and heavy, as is the practice here in town. Some critics say that Kansas City barbecue is a lot like Memphis barbecue, only with a heck of a lot more sauce on it.

As I'm eating Spears informs me, "All of our sauce is made right here in the restaurant and it is stocked in all the major grocery stores here in Kansas City. We have an Internet site where you can order it . . . and we ship it outside of Kansas City." Spears may not ship his pork and brisket by mail like some of the other shops do, but his sauce is making its way from coast to coast.

In spite of its growing reputation in town and nationwide, Hayward's Pit still remains true to its family-style way of doing business. Spears' partner is his wife Hattie, who handles the banquets and catering. His brother Albert has been the pitmaster for the past 30 years. His grandson Kyle is being groomed to take the operation into franchising some day, but that's a long way off. First, he has to finish school. Later, when he's ready—and if he decides to pick up the mantle of his grandfather's business—he'll learn his most important lessons at the pits, discerning the subtle nuances of cooking and when to retrieve meat from their chambers.

At Hayward's they serve six or seven meat products, including beef (the main one), pork spareribs, turkey breast, pit ham, chicken, sausage, and baby-back ribs. The side dishes consist of homemade baked beans, homemade potato salad, and homemade coleslaw. They also serve sweet-potato fries and French fries. ©2008 Michael Karl Witzel

At Hayward's Pit, the open-pit cooking tradition started with Hayward Spears' dad back in Arkansas. To celebrate the Fourth of July holiday, his father would barbecue a whole pig. He'd start on a Friday afternoon and cook all night. By late Saturday, the meat was ready and on Sunday it was served to friends and family. Today, the family-friendly dining continues at Hayward's. ©2008 Michael Karl Witzel

"I can walk in the kitchen and open the door and have our pitmaster doing the cooking and I can just look at the meat and tell if it should be taken off now or should have been taken out 30 minutes ago, or an hour ago," brags Hayward. "I don't have to take a fork and probe it to tell if it's done. I had this awareness from day one, but as the years have gone by, it has grown. I think it's a lot like being a professional athlete—there are just some things they do that just can't be taught."

And to that bold statement, I can only agree. Each of the barbecue masters that I have met in Kansas City is blessed with individual talents and holds claim to their own unique spin on preparing and serving barbecue. That's what is so appealing about visiting so many joints and trying so many different styles of barbecue: every master of the art interprets 'cue their own way and paints the canvas according to their own vision. Whether that vision is realist, surrealist abstract, impressionist, or primitive—it's all good.

"In my judgment, barbecue is not a science, it is an art," Hayward tells me, as if imparting to me one of the great, unknown secrets of the cosmos. "I will stand by that 'til the day I die." But I was already aware of this simple maxim that energizes foodies trapped within barbecue's orbit. Mr. Spears—and Hayward's Pit Bar B Que—merely confirms my knowledge. I thank him and excuse myself to meet the scheduled demands of my barbecue tour.

FIORELLA'S JACK STACK BARBECUE, HOLMES ROAD With my appetite stoked, I'm eager to sample yet another approach to Kansas City barbecue and further expand my appreciation for its many splendored ways. Time flies when you're having great ribs and dinner is on the horizon. For that, my barbecue card is filled and my next destination already prequalified: Fiorella's Jack Stack. During my brief stay in the City of Fountains, I've heard a lot about a specialty called "burnt ends" and aim to find out what all the buzz is about.

I crank up the Fatboy and carefully retrace my path to 435, where I fight lane upon lane of oversized trucks, teens yakking on cell phones, and minivans making their way back to the fast food communities that spawned them. Exiting on Holmes Road, I start to worry that I'm lost—this area doesn't look like a place for Kansas City barbecue. A few miles and one railroad crossing later, my perseverance is rewarded by the sight of a large smokestack and the Fiorella name, done up in bright red plastic letters.

I park the bike among a sea of minivans and SUVs and make a beeline for the front door. There, I'm greeted by the head and the horns of the company's signature bull head, etched into the glass. Inside, the muted lighting, wood finishes, and inlaid Buffalo-brand bricks in the floor are my first clue that this ain't no joint, but a restaurant with a touch of class.

Case Dorman, the president and general manager, welcomes me and treats me to a grand tour. In 1978, he started working at the Stack when he was 16—washing dishes, busing tables, and doing myriad other tasks that nobody else wanted to do. Back then, he didn't have any idea that he would get into the barbecue business. That is until he met Jennifer, his future wife. It just so happened she was the daughter of the owner, Jack Fiorella.

A gleaming rack of cooked pork shoulder is removed from one of the ovens at Jack Stack Barbecue and awaits preparation. From here, the succulent meat will be made into pork sandwiches and other entrées. ©2008 Michael Karl Witzel

Pork ribs are an all-time favorite among Kansas Citians despite the fact that beef rules in this town. Preening for the camera at Fiorella's Jack Stack Barbecue, these beauties are nearing completion and are ready to serve. ©2008 Michael Karl Witzel

Nevertheless, Case had plans of his own and went on to earn a degree in computer technology. But his life's path was still bent by the gravity of the business. "After I came back from college, I started working the cash register in the evenings and suddenly realized that my passion was here," he admits. "So, I found myself running from my day job every afternoon to get back to the restaurant, because I really loved it. In 1987, the year after we got married, I started back at the restaurant again, as a general manager."

Case's father and mother-in-law first purchased the building back in 1974. When Jack and Dolores Fiorella bought the place, it was just another barbecue joint. No one really remembers what the name of it was. They refurbished the place to their own specifications, upgrading the exterior with a green mansard-style roof and cedar-shake siding.

Arthur Bryant's Burnt Ends

1 (8–10 pound) beef brisket
Favorite spice rub
Favorite barbecue sauce (recommended: Arthur Bryant's Rich and Spicy Sauce)

Prepare smoker for cooking, heating to 180 to 200 degrees.

Season brisket with spice rub on both sides then place in smoker. Smoke for 8 hours. Remove brisket to a platter and leave smoker on.

Cut burnt ends (blackened portion) from lean section of smoked brisket and then chop into cubes. Place chopped pieces in a large pan with holes. Smoke for 1-1/2 hours, or until dried out. Remove pan from smoker and transfer brisket cubes to a large pan without any holes. Stir in favorite BBQ sauce, then return to the smoker for an additional 1-1/2 hours. Burnt ends may be combined with baked beans or served on a sandwich.

SOURCE: RECIPE COURTESY OF CHARLES LEE/WWW.COOKS.COM

Above: A horned bull is the logo of Fiorella's Jack Stack Barbecue, etched into the entry door to remind Kansas Citians exactly what their barbecue is all about. ©2008 Michael Karl Witzel

Below: Pitmaster Tommy Kupczyk adds wood to the grill where Jack Stack entrées such as grilled salmon and shish kebobs are prepared. Fiorella's is a full-service restaurant, offering a variety of seafood dishes along with the barbecue. ©2008 Michael Karl Witzel

A friendly pig carving greets you when you enter Fiorella's Jack Stack. During the nineteenth century, pigs were a low-maintenance food source that could be released to forage for themselves in forests or woodlands. When food supplies dwindled, these semi-wild pigs could then be caught and eaten. ©2008 Michael Karl Witzel

Russell Fiorella, Jack's father, originally got the family going in the barbecue business. His kinfolk were farmers over in Jackson County, and during the Great Depression he decided to earn his keep by going into the grocery business. When supermarket chains like Piggly Wiggly began to take over the market, he bailed out and in 1957 opened a small barbecue place on 79th and Prospect in Kansas City called the Smoke Stack.

As always seems to happen in the restaurant business, one party gets to thinking about how they can make things better, while the other wants to keep things the same. In this story, the one who wanted to make changes was Jack Fiorella, who left the Smokestack in 1974 to open his own restaurant. The result was located in Martin City and bore his personal stamp: "Jack Stack."

It's a fascinating story, but I'm chomping at the bit to find out more about one of their premier menu items: the burnt ends. Case leads me to the huge brick ovens at the rear of the

At Fiorella's Jack Stack, the burnt ends are cooked ever so slowly in a rotisserie-style oven where they turn delicious shades of caramel, chocolate brown, and dark umber. ©2008 Michael Karl Witzel

Jack Stack pitmaster Tommy Kupczyk tends to various cuts of meat cooking in the pit. Inside, pork shoulder and racks of ribs are nearing completion. On the rack below, a huge tub of barbecued beans is infused with the smoke and flavor of the oven. ©2008 Michael Karl Witzel

At Fiorella's Jack Stack, the "Hickory Pit Beans" are cooked in the barbecue oven along with the meats. Pieces of meat are mixed in for added flavor. This process gives the beans a full-bodied taste that is impossible to duplicate using any other method. ©2008 Michael Karl Witzel

A tiered tower of golden, hand-battered onion rings is a crowd-pleaser at Fiorella's Jack Stack. ©2008 Michael Karl Witzel

kitchen area and shows me how it's done. "During the 1950s and 1960s, the beef briskets were pretty large, and generally came with the deckle on, which is the thick layer of fat on the underside of the brisket itself," he explains. "Everything was cooked in huge brick ovens over an open flame. Not as much attention was given to the process as it is today, leading to some of the product being overcooked and too tender to slice for a sandwich. So, Grandpa chopped them into cubes of beef and sold them as burnt ends."

Seared on the outside and quite tender on the inside, burnt ends are actually "repurposed" beef brisket. Today, the cubes of smoky goodness are one of the most popular items, both on the menu and for mail order (Jack Stack has a separate 40,000-square-foot facility for mail orders). This is true Kansas City fare—you just won't find burnt ends that can match the flavor of the K.C. variety in Texas, Memphis, or North Carolina joints.

As I greedily snack on a sample covered with sauce, my eyes connect with another dish being prepared. Like the cartoon

In anticipation of the dinner rush, large racks of pork ribs and some Crown Prime Beef short ribs await preparation in the Jack Stack Barbecue kitchen. ©2008 Michael Karl Witzel

One taste of Jack Stack's Hickory Pit Beans will make you wonder how you survived so many years without them. It's all here: bits of real meat and a barbecue flavor that can come only from real pit cooking. ©2008 Michael Karl Witzel

character whose eyes pop out on elastic tendrils and then snap back into their sockets, I'm wowed at what I see: three massive ribs of exquisitely well-marbled beef, presented with hickory pit beans and garnish on an oversized stainless-steel platter. "These are Crown Prime Beef short ribs," Case tells me, "a luxurious delicacy prized by epicures."

I'm eager to sample these beefy monsters post haste. A few minutes later, I'm set up at a secluded back table, piled high with pretty much everything they make at Jack Stack, including grilled fish, an amazing tower of onion rings, pork ribs, corn pudding, and more. But I only have eyes for those short ribs! Just one bite provides a mental picture of their seasoned ovens, the hickory and oak used for fuel, and the obvious high quality of the meat. The total essence of Jack Stack—and the meaning of barbecue—is contained within the marbled meat and the charred "bark" of the exterior.

Case gives me some insight as to why the ribs taste so good. "The average length of tenure for a pitmaster in our stores is

Above: Covered with thick, Kansas City–style barbecue sauce (Jack Stack makes their own KC Original and KC Spicy sauces), a trio of Crown Prime Beef short ribs are served on a stainless-steel platter with a crock of Hickory Pit Beans. ©2008 Michael Karl Witzel

Opposite: Pork ribs and brisket are fine, but once you try a plate of the Crown Prime Beef short ribs at Fiorella's Jack Stack Barbecue you will never go back. The exterior bark, succulent texture of the meat, and sublime smokiness are unmatched. ©2008 Michael Karl Witzel

Jack Stack Denver Lamb Ribs

4 each "Denver cut" lamb spareribs (7–8 ribs/1–2 lbs per slab)
NAMP #209D spring lamb less than nine months old
Available at your local butcher or meat purveyor
4 teaspoons Jack Stack Meat & Poultry Rub (or other favorite rub)

Completely thaw lamb ribs (if frozen). Lightly season meat side of slab with 1 teaspoon of rub. Place slabs, meat side down, on grill directly over hickory or charcoal fire. Sear meat side only until golden brown. Approximately 10 minutes.

Remove ribs from direct heat and place on a cooler spot on your grill to finish cooking the ribs with indirect heat. If available, you may also place the ribs at this point in a slow smoker or rotisserie oven to finish cooking. Finish cooking ribs at 260 degrees for approximately 1 hr and 20 minutes. Lamb ribs are ready when they reach approximately 180 degrees and you can easily push a finger through the meat of thickest part of the slab.

When finished cooking, place on sheet pan or plate in a single layer and allow to cool. Serve with Jack Stack Barbecue Spicy Sauce or your local favorite barbecue sauce.

SOURCE: COURTESY OF JACK STACK BARBECUE, KANSAS CITY, MISSOURI

81

Fiorella's Jack Stack Barbecue general manager Vince Franz takes a quiet moment to himself after the lunch rush, preparing for the dinner time crunch to follow. ©2008 Michael Karl Witzel

As he explains the many intricacies of barbecue cooking, Arthur Bryant's pitmaster Efrem Echols slices up some hot 'cue straight from the pit. ©2008 Michael Karl Witzel

Buffalo Wings Kansas City Style

5 pounds wings, tips removed and separate at the joint
1/2 cup orange juice
2 jalapeño peppers, seeded and diced
3 large cloves of garlic
2 cups red wine vinegar
3/4 teaspoon salt
1/2 teaspoon pepper
2 cups salad oil

Marinade
Combine everything but the oil in a blender. Put blender on low and very slowly add the oil (if you don't do this slowly the oil will separate later). Put the wings in a gallon size freezer zipper bag, pour in marinade. Let the wings marinate overnight.

Dry Rub
6 tablespoons Chili powder
4 tablespoons ground cumin
1–1/2 teaspoons cayenne pepper
Mix ingredients well and pour into a shaker.

Preheat oven to 425 degrees. Drain wings and place in a large pan, packed tight. Sprinkle liberally with the dry rub. Place in oven for about 15–25 minutes. Remove from oven and drain and refrigerate until ready to serve.

Sauce
2 cups canned chicken broth
1/2 cup honey
1–1/4 tablespoons chili powder
1 teaspoon cayenne pepper
1 tablespoon cornstarch
1 cup water

Place broth, honey, chili powder, and cayenne in a saucepan and bring to a boil. Reduce by 1/3. Mix cornstarch with a little water, and add slowly to the boiling sauce; lower temperature. Continue cooking until thick enough to coat with a spoon, usually about 10–15 minutes.

Serving
Preheat broiler or grill. If placing under the broiler put wings on a large cookie sheet and brush them with the sauce. Place under the broiler until hot and crispy. (Ribs will almost char on the tips from the honey.) Heat the remaining sauce on the stove top and serve with the wings as a dip.

Yield: 40 servings

Source: Courtesy of Virginia Dunn

Kansas City Barbecued Brisket

5 pounds brisket of beef
1/4 cup liquid smoke
3 medium onions, chopped
1 garlic clove, peeled and halved
Salt and freshly ground pepper (add to taste)
3 tablespoons brown sugar
16-ounce bottle ketchup
1/2 cup water
2 tablespoons Worcestershire sauce
1 tablespoon dry mustard or 1-1/2 tablespoons Dijon mustard
2 teaspoons celery seasoning (optional)
6 tablespoons Pareve margarine

Wash and dry the brisket and sprinkle with 2 tablespoons of the liquid smoke. Wrap in heavy-duty aluminum foil and marinate overnight. The next day open the foil, sprinkle on the chopped onions, garlic, and pepper. Rewrap everything in the foil and bake in a preheated 325-degree oven for 5 hours.

Meanwhile, combine the remaining 2 tablespoons liquid smoke, the brown sugar, ketchup, water, Worcestershire sauce, mustard, celery seasoning, margarine, and salt and pepper. Simmer, uncovered, for about 30 minutes. Remove the foil, slice the brisket thinly, and pour the sauce over all. Raise the oven to 350 degrees and reheat, covered, for 30 minutes.

Yield: 10 servings

SOURCE: RECIPE COURTESY OF JOAN NATHAN, "THE JEWISH HOLIDAY BAKER" AND "JEWISH COOKING IN AMERICA". RECIPE BY "COOKING LIVE SHOW" (#CL9033) POSTED TO MC-RECIPE DIGEST BY "ANGELE AND JON FREEMAN" (JFREEMAN@COMTECK.COM) ON FEBRUARY 7, 1998

The secret to making beans that go perfectly with the meat is to add the same flavors to it. In Kansas City, the beans have a sweet, smoky flavor, just like the sauce. ©2008 Michael Karl Witzel

Above: Longtime Arthur Bryant's employee Connie Trent fills small containers with barbecue sauce to satisfy the innumerable "to-go" orders that pour in hour after hour. The sweet, tomato-rich sauces like those sold at Arthur Bryant's are typical of the Kansas City barbecue region. ©2008 Michael Karl Witzel

Inset: "Quality is Our Hobby" and "Honesty is Our Policy" were the slogans used by Baugh's Barbecue advertised on this vintage linen Curt Teich postcard. As early as the 1920s and 1930s, the barbecue traditions of regions like Kansas City, Missouri, were being exported to surrounding states, with believers spreading the gospel of 'cue wherever they could. *Author's collection*

about 15 years," he states. "All of our pitmasters train under existing pitmasters to gain the skill set needed and perfect their technique. To become a pitmaster at Jack Stack, you have to go through . . . the full kitchen training program. It can take years to become a really good pitmaster."

Speaking of time, Case looks at his watch and realizes that he's late for an appointment. I linger for another 45 minutes until my stomach is very near bursting. With no wheelchair available to ferry me out to my motorcycle, I heave myself up from my chair and slowly exit. I have a few leftovers and stock my saddlebags with the booty.

As I return to my hotel for the night, the clickety-clack of the joints in the concrete highway lulls my mind into a state of reflection. I think about what Case said to me when I asked him why barbecue is loved by so many: "There's something about the scent and the flavor of meat that is being cooked over the open flame, something so primitive, but so vital that it excites your taste buds. It is the *simplicity* of the flavor profile that appeals to just about everybody."

In the final analysis, simplicity is one of the keys to Kansas City barbecue. The African-Americans who built up the barbecue industry here in town—from virtually nothing—know that. Using basic cuts of meat and a few off-the-shelf ingredients found in any kitchen larder, they created a genre of food that can hold its own with the world's finest culinary dishes.

They have proven that a piece of meat can be a meal in itself, without the aid of fancy bread crusts, complex gravies, and hours of marinating. They have also shown me that a barbecue place doesn't always have to be a joint or a shack on the tracks. Barbecue can be dignified, refined.

I turn out the lights and dream of the great places that I've experienced like Hayward's Pit Bar B Que, Gates Bar-B-Q, and Jack Stack. Tomorrow, I'm trading my motorcycle for a friend's 1957 Chevrolet and heading south, leaving "The Barbecue Capital of the World" in Missouri to explore yet another capital. This time, it's Memphis, Tennessee . . . known to many as the "The Pork Barbecue Capital of the World."

After Arthur Bryant passed away in 1982, Gary Berbiglia and Bill Rauschelbach acquired the restaurant. Together, they expanded the business while preserving Arthur Bryant's traditions and world-famous flavor. Arthur used to mix and store his sauce in 5-gallon glass jars. You can still see one in the window of the Brooklyn Avenue restaurant today. As Gary Berbiglia puts it, "It's history." ©2008 Michael Karl Witzel

After World War II, the typical barbecue place was nothing more than a "shack by the track." Ramshackle structures like this corrugated-metal example, seen circa 1944, occupied land where property values were low. *Russell Lee, Library of Congress*

Barbecue Bob Blues

Robert Hicks was born on September 11, 1902, in Walnut Grove, Georgia. After his parents moved to Newton County, he joined his older brother Charlie in taking guitar lessons from local guitar-picking diva Savannah "Dip" Weaver. Both brothers made friends with the young Weaver boy, "Curley," and soon they were practicing their pentatonic scales together.

By the time Hicks learned his licks, he had begun working at Tidwell's Barbecue in Buckhead, where he cooked food and served customers. As the meat smoked, his fingers fried the frets and sizzled the strings. The customers loved his hard-driving style so much that he was often invited to after-hours parties, where he continued to flaunt his infectious rhythm.

Never mind dealing with the devil at the crossroads—Hicks was becoming a blues sensation by way of pulled pork. When Columbia Records scout Dan Hornsby brought his recording team through Atlanta, he crossed paths with Hicks and was duly impressed by the sound of his clear and articulate tenor.

Hornsby needed a hook to market the unknown blues artist, so he decided to use Hick's day job as a gimmick. To capitalize on the barbecue tie-in, Hicks was photographed dressed in chef's whites (complete with chef's hat) and dubbed "Barbecue Bob." On March 25, 1927, his very first record for Columbia was recorded. It was given the tasty title of—what else—"Barbecue Blues."

As it turned out, the promotional idea charmed fans better than black cat bone. Soon, his record was blaring from juke joints and barbecue pits across the Deep South. Over the next three years, Bob refined his chops and recorded for Columbia whenever they rolled their recording truck through Atlanta. All total, he cut some 62 sides for the label.

Backed by the full sound of his Stella 12-string, Barbecue Bob emerged as one of the reigning raconteurs of 1920s "race records." His "Motherless Chile Blues" (a standard covered by guitarist Eric Clapton) became well-known. By the 1930s, his inventive playing technique had helped him gain a wide audience.

But like many great blues singers of legend, he experienced his own bout of trouble during the Great Depression. Hard times hit the recording industry and jinxed the growth of blues and country music. As he struggled to hone his musical avocation, Bob's mother passed away, followed by the untimely death of his wife just one year later.

On October 21, 1931, Hicks joined the heavenly choir himself, passing from this earthly realm of barbecue and blues by way of pneumonia. At the age of 29, Atlanta's Barbecue Bob, onetime pitmaster who became a popular Southern bluesman, was gone. He left behind a recorded legacy of Barbecue Blues, and memories of some great tasting 'cue.

A mural near Arthur Bryant's in Kansas City commemorates the blues and the heyday of 18th Street and Vine. ©2008 Michael Karl Witzel

Kansas City Grease House Rosedale Bar-B-Q

600 Southwest Boulevard
Kansas City, Kansas 66103
(913) 262-0343

If there is one thing Kansas City does not lack, it's barbecue joints. With more than 100 barbecue-specific restaurants cranking out the 'cue, this city wails with more varieties of sauce than a saxophone has valves. It's a rich melding of smoke, with overtones of jazz—and a culture that's reflected in its mouth-watering blend of spicy and sweet sauce.

Kansas City also boasts some of the longest-standing restaurants around. One such survivor sits on the Kansas side of Kansas City in an area once known for its neighborly ways and its predilection for cold brew. When you mix brew with smoke and jazz, you have a decided hit on your hands. That's exactly what Anthony Rieke intended when he opened up the little barbecue shack that became the place called Rosedale Bar-B-Q.

In 1934, the Great Depression was nipping at the nation's heels, and Kansas City was not totally immune to its bite. Struggling to make a living, two men—Anthony Rieke and his brother-in-law, Anthony Sieleman—hit upon the idea to sell beer and hot dogs out of a former root beer stand. It was the beginning of an adventure that would span decades.

At first, beer was the partnership's primary mover and shaker. The enterprise, appropriately named "The Bucket Shop," specialized in beer by the bucketload at a quarter a bottle. "You bring the bucket and we'll fill it," was their sales motto. The trouble was that people wanted beer, but few had even a quarter to their name. So, sometimes the partners would accept beans and flour in exchange for some suds.

In the meantime, the partners became aware of a place called Fatty Sharp's, a little shanty down by the City Market that sold smoked meat. It was the heavenly smell of cured beef wafting through the air that finally drove them into the barbecue business. The health department shut down The Bucket Shop because of improper waste management. Unfazed, the partners scraped together $183 and in 1936 opened up Rosedale Bar-B-Q. It was just a shack, only 12 by 16 feet in size, and barely large enough to accommodate a restaurant.

Fortunately, what they had in mind was a simple carry-out facility. Customers would drive up and wait for an order in their car. Back then, carry-out accouterments did not exist, so the to-go slab of barbecued ribs was wrapped in newspaper.

To help production, Rieke—a man with no lack of ideas—designed and built a simple hand-cranked rotisserie. Business took off and in 1949 the dining room was expanded to accommodate more customers. By the 1950s, Rosedale Bar-B-Q was hitting its stride and the simple hand-cranked rotisserie could no longer keep up with demand. Rieke decided to design a larger, automated unit and spent every spare moment working on the new gadget at his family farm in Shawnee, Kansas.

When it was finished, he had a problem: how could he test the machine without burning up expensive meat? After all, he needed to make certain the unit would hold the slabs of ribs and run smoothly.

(continued overleaf)

Marisha Smith, the granddaughter of Rosedale Bar-B-Q founder Anthony Rieke, is the current owner and operator of this long-time Kansas City barbecue haven. Her specialty item is pork ribs, an entrée that still packs in the customers after more than 60 years in operation. ©2008 Michael Karl Witzel

The atmosphere at Rosedale Bar-B-Q is a lot like a friendly neighborhood bar. No pretense or formalities here. You can hang out on one of the diner-style barstools and have a beer, or take a table and concentrate on the ribs. ©2008 Michael Karl Witzel

Opened in 1934, Rosedale Bar-B-Q has become a neighborhood fixture in Kansas City. Today, the large restaurant, with its neighborhood bar–type atmosphere, is a favorite after-work meeting place. ©2008 Michael Karl Witzel

As Marisha, Rieke's granddaughter explains, "He had to figure out if it was going to cook things slowly and evenly and whether it was going to have the balance it needed. He was a fairly petite man and so he figures he's going to crawl into this thing. And so, he rode it like a carousel and said, 'It's the most fun I ever had working!' He just rode that thing like it was a carnival ride!" Reike's rotisserie was used until 1991, when they moved into their new building.

In those early days, there were only a handful of barbecue restaurants in the area. Since then, many more have opened and closed, while some have made a name for themselves in the marketplace. But none has captured the heart of locals like Rosedale Bar-B-Q. Over the years, it has served customers from all walks of life, including hobos, news crews, businessmen, blue-collar workers, and even a United States President.

Here, ribs are the highlight. When they say "slab," they really mean it! Their ample racks exhibit a mouth-watering texture that's difficult to match. Mind you, this is not a feast for the calorie-minded patron. Indeed, the meat is well-marbled with fat. This fact, plus the slow-cooked process, is what creates a succulence difficult to beat. But don't expect stellar side-dish performance here: Rosedale puts all of its energy into the meat of the matter which—when you come right down to it—is what matters the most.

Family tradition continues to this day with granddaughter Marisha Smith in charge. Marisha began her full-time training behind the

Made with tomato ketchup, tomato paste, spices (this is where the secret recipe comes into play), vinegar, and salt, Rosedale Bar-B-Q Sauce has no preservatives added. Packaged in brown-labeled plastic bottles, it comes in a variety of sizes, ready to take home. Rich and thick barbecue sauce (with molasses) rose to fame in Kansas City, spurred on in 1977 by K.C. Masterpiece inventor Rich Davis. ©2008 Michael Karl Witzel

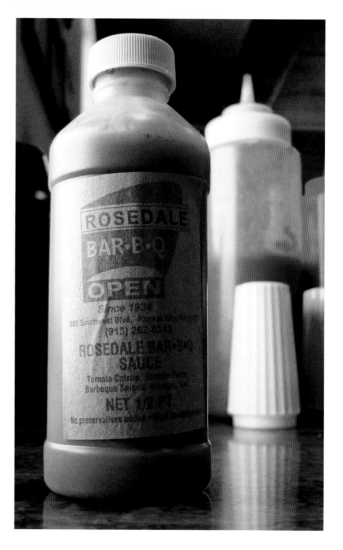

counter at the age of 22, and her mother, Janelle Brown, joined the ranks back in the early 1980s. According to Janelle, the pricing policy of "Give the customers the best quality food at the lowest possible price" is one good thing that came out of the Depression days.

In a 1994 interview, she stated that Rosedale was "careful not to charge too much for the product so everybody can afford them. I think some of that comes from the Depression when it was important to share." Pricing and friendly service, not to mention the almost-legendary status of the place, has garnered Rosedale a place in the annals of Kansas City barbecue history and, most importantly, in the hearts of its loyal customers.

It's been over 70 years since those hurly-burly days when the two original partners joined in a venture that would take them into unknown territory. If they could see how the community has been enriched by the presence of this place, and how over 1,000 customers come in every day to order a slab of ribs, they would no doubt be proud.

Above: At Rosedale Bar-B-Q, the recipe for a burnt end sandwich is simple: Ignacio Vaca piles a mound of barbecued beef cubes on a piece of Wonder Bread and covers it with plenty of sauce. Add another slice of white bread and, voilà, it's ready to eat. ©2008 Michael Karl Witzel

Left: The thick tomato base of Kansas City–style barbecue sauce is often sweetened with molasses or brown sugar. Depending on the peppers and spices added, its flavor can range from mild to wild. Here, large tubs of sauce await final preparation in the Rosedale Bar-B-Q kitchen. ©2008 Michael Karl Witzel

At Rosedale Bar-B-Q, customers may partake of a combination platter featuring the best of both worlds: barbecued ribs and chicken, along with beans and coleslaw. RC Cola is a favorite soft drink in this region, a perfect accompaniment to the smoked meats. ©2008 Michael Karl Witzel

CHAPTER 3

Memphis

SLOW-SMOKED AND BASTED WITH BLUES

70

64

Above: Interstate Bar-B-Que was rated as the second-best barbecue in the nation by *People* magazine in 1989. *Vogue* magazine proclaimed it the best commercial barbecue in Memphis. And after a two-month search of numerous restaurants in Memphis, *The Commercial Appeal* named Interstate as the home of the best all-around pork barbecue sandwich in the city in 1989. ©*2008 Michael Karl Witzel*

Right: In 1956, Jax Brewing Company sold the Jax Beer copyright to Jackson Brewing Company in New Orleans. The brand changed hands again when the Jackson Brewing Company closed in 1974. Pearl Brewing Company in San Antonio, Texas, acquired the rights to the Jax beer formula and label. *Library of Congress*

WITH B. B. KING'S "THE THRILL IS GONE" oozing from the chrome grille of my '57 Chevrolet's dashboard speaker, I'm cruising south toward Memphis, Tennessee, on Highway 61, the "Blues Highway," exploring the sad, forgotten rooms of America, through fields of cotton, past abandoned gin joints, shotgun shacks, forsaken motels, and the skeletons of gas stations—rolling past the small towns and people unmoved by the twentieth century.

Opposite: A trio of large, hickory-smoked pork-shoulder sandwiches wait in the pass-through window of Neely's Interstate Bar-B-Q, summing up what the Memphis barbecue experience is all about. Who in their right mind could resist taking a big bite out of one of these beauties? ©*2008 Michael Karl Witzel*

My destination is Memphis, Tennessee, a city of the Mid-South known from coast-to-coast for "Elvis, Blues, and Barbecue," but not necessarily in that order. It's the home of founders of various American music genres, including blues, gospel, rock 'n' roll, and "sharecropper" country music. During the 1950s, Johnny Cash, Elvis Presley, and B. B. King—dubbed the "Kings" of country, rock 'n' roll, and blues, respectively—all got their start here. Memphis is also one of the four vital

Opposite: At the Mount Moriah (Fox Plaza Drive) location of Leonard's Pit Barbecue, the proprietors offer cafeteria-style, all-you-can-eat service during the day. Customers can pile their plates high with all kinds of barbecue, including the ever-popular Memphis favorite, pork ribs. ©2008 Michael Karl Witzel

Right: Tops is a Memphis, Tennessee, chain with at least a dozen locations. Their specialty is the pulled-pork sandwich, an item many Memphians choose to eat over fast food hamburgers. *Author's collection*

Below: At Tops, they still respect the integrity of the pig and cook the old-fashioned way: using hardwood charcoal and real green hickory wood. Pork shoulders are cooked over an open-pit fire for 8 to 10 hours, depending on their size. ©2008 Michael Karl Witzel

regions of American barbecue, a city that's billed as "The Pork Barbecue Capital of the World."

With that slogan in mind, I admit to myself that, yes, I'm hungry once again and ready, willing, and able to dig into what I know is this region's most venerated specialty: barbecued pig. As the final licks from B. B.'s guitar, Lucille, fade into another blues tune, I connect with the freeway and resign myself to the fact that my trip through America's yesterday has drawn to a close. As the tires click out their own steady rhythm, I soon reach the banks of the Mississippi River and am ferried across the watery divide by way of the Hernando De Soto Bridge, know by some locals as the "Dolly Parton" bridge, due to its distinctive architecture.

While leading the first European expedition into the territory of the modern-day United States, conquistador and Spanish explorer De Soto "discovered" the Mississippi River. Yet even more important to barbecue-crazy Memphians, he's the figure responsible for the introduction of pigs to the South. When he landed in Florida in 1539, he brought a whole herd of feral swine with him.

A&R Bar-B-Que is as unpretentious as Memphis barbecue gets. There are no flat-panel televisions or even jukeboxes here. A half-dozen diner stools and a few small tables provide a cozy atmosphere. ©2008 Michael Karl Witzel

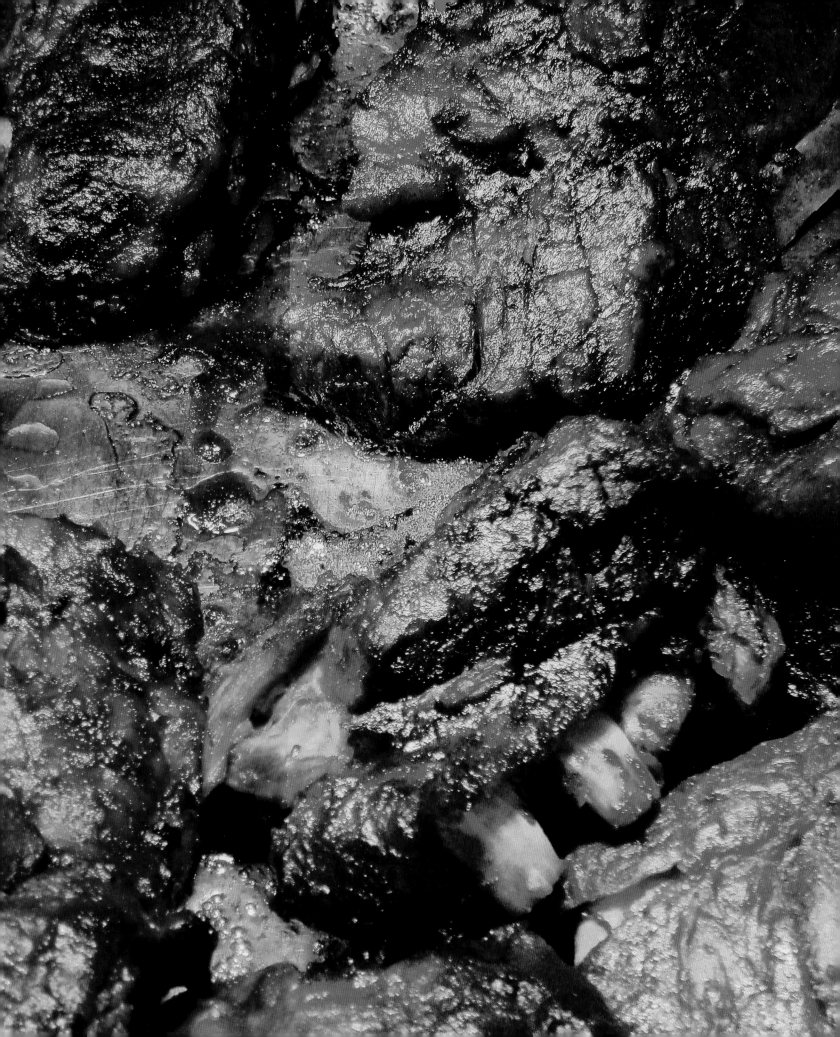

As I traverse the span, I contemplate the immense pyramid built on the other side to commemorate this town's Egyptian namesake. How many hogs could fit inside, I wonder? Not the loftiest thought, I grant you, but appropriate if you consider that after you cross Old Muddy, you can catch the sweet aroma of barbecue smoke on almost every street corner. With over 100 joints, shacks, diners, dives, and yes—restaurants—doing business in the city alone, even established fast food chains are getting a run for their money.

Here, barbecue *is* fast food, proven by the likes of the local chain called "Tops," which takes on contenders like McDonald's on a daily basis. How can the McRib sandwich stand up to the one-two punch of real, wood smoked 'cue? It can't, and you would be met with deafening silence if you asked any of the town's learned pitmasters this inane question.

Leaving the De Soto Bridge, I turn right on Main Street and eyeball the trolley cars, horse-drawn carriages, and interesting people that paint the city with life. A few stop lights later, I cross Beale Street, the "Home of the Blues," and glance up at the guitar-shaped sign of B. B. King's Blues Club. King was once a disc jockey at WDIA, one of the first black-staffed and managed stations in Memphis. He called himself the "Beale Street Blues Boy," a title that he later shortened to "Blues Boy King" and then down to his famous initials. My tour book clues me in to the fact that B. B.'s club also serves pulled pork and ribs.

That's no surprise, since blues and barbecue have been joined at the blade bone ever since the guitar first got strings. In their heyday, it wasn't unusual for juke joints to pay musicians in

Above: Barbecue pioneer James W. Lawson started the Tops Bar-B-Q dynasty in 1952 next to a store out on Macon Road and turned it into a Memphis fixture. Today, the flagship shop is gone, but the independent chain still counts 11 units citywide. Tops is a reminder that barbecue is king in Elvis town, where people with a penchant for pork are more apt to sink their teeth into "a hunk of burnin' 'cue" than any other food. ©2008 Michael Karl Witzel

Opposite: In 1998, the Tops Bar-B-Q eatery was awarded the bronze medal for the "Best Barbecue Sandwich" in Memphis by the *Restaurant Guide*. Some say the wife of German-Jewish barbecue entrepreneur Leonard Heuberger was the genius behind the addition of coleslaw on a pulled-pork sandwich. While her husband was out running errands, she was running low on 'cue. To stretch it out, she decided to put slaw on the sandwiches. It proved to be an instant hit with customers, so it stayed. ©2008 Michael Karl Witzel

John Wills Bar-B-Que Bar and Grill Memphis Barbecue Sauce

1 (8-ounce) can tomato sauce
1/2 cup spicy honey mustard
1 cup catsup
1 cup red wine vinegar
1/2 cup Worcestershire sauce
1/4 cup butter or margarine
2 tablespoons hot sauce
1 tablespoon lemon juice
2 tablespoons brown sugar
1 tablespoon paprika
1 tablespoon seasoned salt
1-1/2 tablespoons garlic powder
1/8 teaspoon chili powder
1/8 teaspoon ground red pepper
1/8 teaspoon black pepper

Combine all ingredients in a Dutch oven. Bring to a boil; reduce heat and simmer 30 minutes, stirring occasionally.

Yields: 1 quart

SOURCE: JOHN WILLS OF JOHN WILLS BAR-B-QUE BAR AND GRILL IN MEMPHIS, TENNESSEE, BY WAY OF WWW.ALL-RESTAURANTRECIPES.COM

Above: The dancing pigs painted on the front door of The Bar-B-Q Shop represent Brady and Lil, the couple from whom Frank Vernon and his wife Hazel learned the recipes and traditions that form the foundation of their Memphis business. ©2008 Michael Karl Witzel

Right: There's nothing like these glowing red letters written in neon tubing to alert the senses to the availability of one of the most flavorful genres of American food. The Bar-B-Q Shop, Memphis, Tennessee. ©2008 Michael Karl Witzel

Opposite: Jim Neely's Interstate Bar-B-Que server Monique Davis prepares to deliver a heaping tray filled with a mouth-watering assortment of barbecue sandwiches, spaghetti, French fries, beef links, and other entrées to customers in the dining area. **Inset:** According to some, sauce is what "separates you from the money." If you can make a good sauce that people really like, you make money in the barbecue business. Leonard's cook and site caterer Lyndell Whitmore pours it on without holding back, just as the customers like it. *Both ©2008 Michael Karl Witzel*

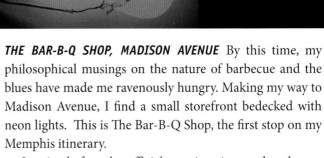

the currency of smoked meat. Eating barbecue while listening to the blues also has no equal. Take the typical 12-bar blues progression, for instance. One knows what to expect when they hear it. The same can be said for barbecue: it might be made a little differently from place to place, but the pleasure is constant. Like the blues, really good barbecue originates from that mysterious place where love crosses desire, bumps into ambition, and burns with passion.

THE BAR-B-Q SHOP, MADISON AVENUE By this time, my philosophical musings on the nature of barbecue and the blues have made me ravenously hungry. Making my way to Madison Avenue, I find a small storefront bedecked with neon lights. This is The Bar-B-Q Shop, the first stop on my Memphis itinerary.

I arrive before the official opening time and make my way to the front door, which is adorned with the images of

Above left: Named after an unknown military hero in 1841, Beale Street acted as General Ulysses S. Grant's headquarters during the Civil War. Its heyday was in the 1920s, when gambling, drinking, prostitution, murder, and voodoo thrived alongside nightclubs, theaters, and restaurants. Long gone, Hambone's Bar-B-Que was one of those businesses. *Author's collection* **Above right:** Frank Vernon's son Eric is learning the ropes at The Bar-B-Q Shop and works right alongside his father. He's poised to take over the operation for the next generation. *©2008 Michael Karl Witzel*

two dancing pigs. Owner Frank Vernon spies me through the glass and comes to the front to unlock and let me in. I enter and my olfactory senses are pleasantly awakened by the lovely aroma emanating from the pits as Frank proceeds to show me around his world and regale me with his knowledge of how to make barbecue.

With a nostalgic look in his eye, he tells me that he and his wife Hazel first took over the reins of this eatery back in 1982. During the 1970s, the couple operated a Holland House chain restaurant over on Scott Street. Like almost all other Memphians, they liked barbecue, even though their short-order menu didn't specialize in it. To get their fix of smoked pork, they frequented a barbecue joint called Brady and Lil's.

"I'd always go in there and ask Mr. Brady about selling the place," Vernon explains. "I was a backyard barbecue guy and I kinda wanted to get into it. I told him if he ever decided that he wanted to retire, I'd like to have the first shot at it. He'd say, 'Well . . . I'm thinking about doing it.' So one day, I came in and I didn't have it on my mind and he suddenly said to me, 'Hey,

look, are you still interested in taking over this restaurant?' I really did, and we began to crunch some numbers. Short time later, I shut down the Holland House restaurant over on Scott Street and was in the barbecue business!"

Known these days as The Bar-B-Q Shop, the former Brady and Lil's boasts 2,400 square feet and 22 employees. The atmosphere inside the 90-year-old building is cozy, with a tin ceiling and a large wooden bar setting the mood. Supposedly, the wooden structure was salvaged from a nearby Catholic church and the mirrors from the confession booths. The top of the bar is layered with a collage of Memphis memorabilia, sealed under a thick layer of acrylic.

We take our conversation to the back and Vernon gives me a tour of the kitchen. The stainless-steel doors of a gleaming Southern Pride cooker swing open to reveal packed racks of perfectly browned meat on their way to becoming Memphis barbecue. Vernon tells me that at his place, the "Boston butt" is the most barbecued cut. "It doesn't have the fat and gristle that you've got to throw away," he explains, pointing to the

Opposite: Frank Vernon runs The Bar-B-Q Shop with his wife Hazel. They purchased it in 1982 when it was called Brady and Lil's Bar-B-Q. Frank and Hazel were customers there and also owned another restaurant at the time called Frank's Restaurant. *©2008 Michael Karl Witzel*

Frank Vernon of The Bar-B-Q Shop checks on pork butts smoking in his pit. The Boston butt is the center cut of the shoulder that doesn't have the weight (the fat and gristle) that you have to throw away. Nor is there much skin, except for a small portion on one side of the cut. ©2008 Michael Karl Witzel

large hunks of meat that are taking a slow Ferris wheel ride inside his cooker. "People go to barbecue places sometimes and they say, 'You don't have any skins? No barbecue skins?' The Boston butt doesn't have any skin on it except the little bit on the backside. The only thing it's got in it is the shank bone. Other than that, you've just one big ol' piece of meat, about two-and-one-half to four full pounds."

According to butchers, the Boston butt is a cut of pork that's taken from the upper part of the shoulder, the front leg. Before the Revolutionary War, New England butchers took cuts of meat that were not highly valued, or "high on the hog," and packed them into casks or barrels. These containers were known as "butts." Over time, the way the hog shoulder was cut in the Boston area became known in other parts of the country as "Boston butt." Why they don't use the term to describe the cut in Boston is anyone's guess.

For barbecue lovers who have never been to Memphis, another important fact to remember about the city's pork barbecue is that the meat isn't cut or sliced to make sandwiches or platters. For that matter, it isn't chopped, minced, or diced either. Here, "pulled pork" is the standard method of preparation, whereby the meat is literally pulled off of the Boston butt or pork shoulder by hand.

Now educated about the different cuts of pork, I'm also pleasantly surprised to find out that Vernon uses the very best meat possible for the brisket he smokes at The Bar-B-Q Shop. "We use a Black Angus beef and have been doing so for almost a year now," he states. "It's working out real well—it's sold even

Out on Elvis Presley Boulevard in Memphis, Tennessee, A&R Barbeque is another one of those corner barbecue shops that enjoys a loyal clientele of local customers. Fair prices and a varied selection are what keep them coming back. ©2008 Michael Karl Witzel

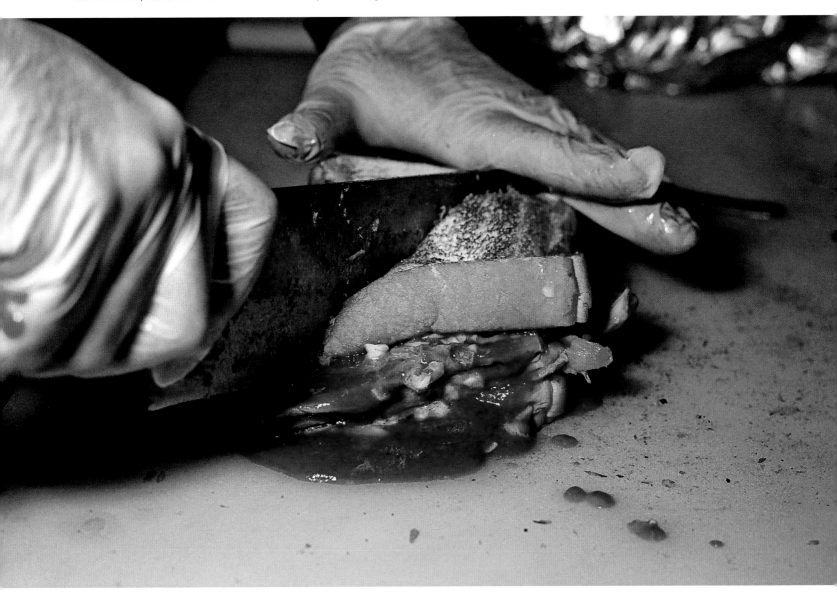

At The Bar-B-Q Shop in Memphis, cook Jeremy slices a sauce-drenched pulled-pork sandwich in two, readying the moist treat for yet another customer.
©2008 Michael Karl Witzel

Above: The bar at The Bar-B-Q Shop is a real conversation piece. The wooden structure came out of the Catholic church years ago and the mirrors were supposedly confession booths. A collection of Memphis memorabilia adorns the bar surface under a layer of acrylic. ©2008 Michael Karl Witzel

Right: Charlie Nickens & Sons was a famous pit barbecue doing business on 305 Jefferson Street in Nashville, Tennessee. Featuring curb service for diners in their cars, their special was a barbecue pork plate for 70 cents, including two vegetables, coleslaw, and corn bread. *Author's collection*

more than the regular, moist brisket. The meat is a lot leaner and more tender. It has some fat, but very little."

Even more interesting is that Vernon isn't afraid to take chances in his kitchen. Besides the usual pork and beef entrées that you would find anywhere else, he also makes a mean plate of barbecue spaghetti. Known worldwide, it's dished up on a platter with pork on one half and spaghetti on the other. Some customers come in just for the pasta, while others get it as a side order to eat with their sandwich. Whatever combination you want, Vernon provides.

"Some people just cook up spaghetti and then pour barbecue sauce on it and say it's barbecue spaghetti," Vernon confides. "To make the real thing, we take a regular pasta with a base that we normally make that's been around for more than 50 years and put it on the pit. Then, we cook it for about seven hours." He opens the door to the pit and shows me the pasta in progress. "See, the base sits over the pit and the drippings from the meat above fall off into the base and flavor it. And then we put it on the original pit up front—the open pit. Anything else I might say might give it away. It's a secret recipe, you know."

The heavy metal door swings closed with a clank as it probably has done a million times before and Vernon motions in the direction of the dining room. "We had Bobby Flay down here about a year and a half ago," Vernon says, referring to the renowned chef and Food Network host, "and he's got all of his cameras and lights set up here and he's asking me, 'Frank, what has it got in it?' He kept trying to guess but couldn't get at what the ingredients were."

"What's so special about the open pit when it comes to making spaghetti?" I ask him. He looks at me in amazement, the way a master might look at a neophyte seeking the answer to a simple question. School is in and this is Barbecue 101. Vernon explains that "the pit is what adds the flavor to the spaghetti. There is no shortcut to it. You just can't get it any other way. When you open the doors to the pit, you get the aroma from just opening them. Inside, they're covered with grease. When I had it built I cured it by mopping it down with fat, meat, and barbecue sauce. Now, the tourists come and want to go back there, open the doors, and smell it!"

Today, Vernon still uses the original charcoal pit as much as he can, but reserves the seasoned smoking chamber for pork ribs. There is a big difference in the quality and the taste, he admonishes me. "One thing about the open pit is that when you start to get your drippings from your ribs, your pork,

or whatever, they drop down into the hot charcoal and then you get that grease that comes right back up. It goes right on through the meat and enhances the flavor."

Cooking meat on the live pit is not really as easy as it looks, although it can be taught. "It's hard to find a real pitmaster," he admits. "And you can't get just anyone to come in and then train them on how to cook on the pit. It's something that a person has to say that they really want to learn. With the pit, you really have to know what you're doing . . . . say you put butts on it for the first hour and then it starts dripping. If you go off and don't watch it, 'BOOM', there go the flames and you have to play fire department!"

The difficulties of live-pit cooking described by Vernon are why a lot of barbecue restaurants have switched over to a popular wood-burning smoker made by Southern Pride.

In 2000, The Bar-B-Q Shop was recognized in Memphis as having the best barbecue sandwich. They put slaw on top of their pulled-pork sandwich, believing that it enhances the sauce and complements the meat. Their slaw is mayonnaise-based and a little sweet, with bell peppers, onions, and carrots. ©2008 Michael Karl Witzel

Located in a strip mall that has seen better days, the second location of Payne's Bar-B-Q caters to a mostly local crowd of customers, but is frequented every so often by pilgrims visiting Memphis in search of great-tasting barbecue. ©2008 Michael Karl Witzel

The Bar-B-Q Shop Bar-B-Q Spaghetti

Cook pasta for 15 minutes and drain. Rinse in cold water and drain.

Meanwhile in a large skillet, add:
1 cup chopped onions
3/4 cup chopped green peppers
1 pint of Dancing Pigs Original Bar-B-Q Sauce
1 cup sugar
2 tablespoons "liquid smoke"
1/2 cup cooking oil
A dash of salt

Stir occasionally and cook slowly for about 30 minutes until onions are translucent and peppers are tender. Pour Bar-B-Q sauce over pasta and stir. Dice up pork shoulder and place on top of each serving. Serve hot.

Serves: 6–8

SOURCE: FRANK VERNON, THE BAR-B-Q SHOP, MEMPHIS, TENNESSEE

Above: Located on Madison Avenue in Memphis, Tennessee, The Bar-B-Q Shop greets customers after dark with its glowing red neon, leading the way to great-tasting 'cue. ©2008 Michael Karl Witzel

Right: Dan Brown (no relation to the Mr. Brown who adorns the neon signs of this establishment) runs the Leonard's Pit Barbecue location on Fox Plaza Drive in Memphis. Like most of the other pits in Memphis, Leonard's is best known for its flavorful pulled pork, shown here piled high on a plate, ready to eat. ©2008 Michael Karl Witzel

Vernon put one in The Bar-B-Q Shop a few years back and finds it invaluable for helping out when his live pit is full. Its chief advantage is that it doesn't have any direct heat or fire under the meat. The hickory wood is held in a patented, air-over-wood firebox and lit by a gas flame. An electrically-powered rotisserie circulates the meat. As it turns, a convection system continually recirculates smoke and heat throughout the pit, smoking the meat.

"Back when I first started I wanted to stay with the original pit, but as the demand goes up, it just can't handle it all," Vernon explains, an apologetic look in his eye. "But everybody can load it up on the Southern Pride. I cook Boston butts on it, beef, and some chicken. I tell you, it really makes a difference because you can put them on at 7:30 and let them cook until the next morning—12 hours—and you don't have to worry about them."

Leonard's Pit Barbecue opened in 1922 when founder Leonard Heuberger bartered a Model T Ford for a seven-stool sandwich stand in South Memphis. In 1932, he moved to a location at 1140 South Bellevue, which he enlarged several times over the years as demand grew for his barbecue food specialties. ©2008 Michael Karl Witzel

Trained by Mr. Brady himself, Vernon still likes to use the live pit to cook ribs and has perfected the art. "You've got a whole pit full of ribs and even if you've got your charcoal spread out evenly, sometimes one side cooks better than the other," he says. "So, you have to know how to move the ones on the left to the right and flip that one over to keep it from overcooking. In the beginning, it took me a couple of months to get it right. You gotta have a passion for it. Because you're saying to yourself, 'Oh I know these didn't turn out right but I have to get back in there and do it.' That's how you become that master—gettin' in there and never giving up. That's it."

Vernon doesn't have to convince me. Just a few bites of his barbecue spaghetti make me a true believer. I admit that, at first, the idea wasn't that appealing to me, but after trying it, I can honestly report that there is nothin' else like it. Fortunately, Mr. Vernon is kind enough to pack me up with leftovers, ensuring that I will have an ample supply once I get back to my hotel room.

Laden down with the best The Bar-B-Q Shop has to offer, I thank Frank Vernon for his time, pass through the door with the dancing pigs, and do a little jig of my own on the way back to the '57 Chevy.

CHARLES VERGOS' RENDEZVOUS, SOUTH SECOND STREET My
next stop in Memphis is Charles Vergos' Rendezvous, a back-alley place that some say is difficult to find. For locals and visitors, alike, the Rendezvous' juicy ribs are what barbecue in Memphis is all about—despite the fact that they are served with nary a drop of sauce.

For three generations, the Rendezvous has been located in the alley, downstairs, behind 52 South Second Street in downtown Memphis, Tennessee. Technically, it's a stone's throw from Maggie H. Isabel Street and General Washburn's Escape Alley, but I dare you to find either on a Google map or a GPS receiver. Save yourself some time and head straight to Allright Central Parking on 153 Monroe Avenue. Once you're parked, it's as easy as slipping out the side gate into the alley alongside the parking garage. The Rendezvous is just a few steps across the alley. Just look for the green building with Old English–style lettering.

Charles Vergos was the King of Ribs in Memphis, popularizing a sauce-less variety that some refer to as "dry-rub style." Today, his moist and flavorful ribs have made the Rendezvous an icon of the Memphis barbecue scene. *Courtesy of John Vergos* **Inset:** Located near the intersection of General Washburn's Escape Alley and Maggie H. Isabel Street, the Rendezvous is not the easiest place to find—especially if you are hungry and eager to sink your teeth into a rack of ribs. ©2008 Michael Karl Witzel

For three generations, the Rendezvous has been located in the alley, downstairs, behind 52 South Second in downtown Memphis. When you come upon the green and red striped awning, you will know you finally found it. ©2008 Michael Karl Witzel

Opposite: With hot charcoal ovens at his back, cook Elliot Brooks takes care of some final rib preparations before they are served. At the Rendezvous, the ribs are pre-sliced for the customer's convenience, after which the signature seasoning is sprinkled on in generous quantities. ©2008 Michael Karl Witzel

The restaurant is subterranean, so you have to take a flight of stairs down to where a hostess greets you. At first glance, the interior decor strikes me as a cross between Bennigan's and the Addams Family. Amid portraits of the founder and other paintings, an eclectic mix of artifacts occupies display cases and is mounted to the walls, including antique toys, Indian arrowheads, movie stills, muskets, swords, vintage whiskey bottles, wooden ship models, and even sheet music signed by the father of the blues himself, W. C. Handy.

I meet John Vergos, who along with brother Nick and sister Tina, runs the restaurant started by the clan patriarch whose name graces the awning, Charles Vergos. John shows me the

There's nothing more macho than gathering up the boys and heading down to the Rendezvous for a full rack of ribs and a couple of bottles of beer. Gnawing on a pork rib conjures up all sorts of primeval emotions. ©2008 Michael Karl Witzel

cooking area, situated immediately to the right of the stairs where customers queue up to wait for their table. It's an open-kitchen arrangement, where customers can watch the cooking process. For a Saturday afternoon, the place is at normal tempo, with cooks, servers, and busboys running about in an orchestrated madness, dodging hot racks of ribs as they take care of business.

It's obvious that these folks have been doing this for quite some time. No sooner does a rack of sizzling ribs fly out of the pit than it's slammed down on the cutting board and sliced into pieces. Next, the celebrated Rendezvous seasoning—a reddish combination of proprietary herbs and spices—is sprinkled onto the ribs in a heavy layer from a big shaker jar. Technically, it's not a dry rub, since it's not rubbed into the meat prior to cooking. Here, the mixture makes contact with the ribs only *after* the meat is done.

Although each bite produces a distinct crackling snap, they are moist and packed with flavor created by the world famous dry rub seasoning developed by founder Charles Vergos. ©2008 Michael Karl Witzel

Charlie Vergos' Rendezvous Restaurant World-Famous Ribs

4 cups distilled white vinegar
4 cups water
1/3 cup Rendezvous Famous Seasoning
2 slabs pork loin back ribs (approximately 2 pounds each)

Mix vinegar, water and seasoning together to make your basting sauce.

Cook meat over direct heat on the grill, approximately 18 inches above fire. Coals should be at 325–360 degrees. Start ribs bone side down, until bone side is golden brown. Baste 2 times with basting sauce then flip slab and cook meat side down until this side reaches a nice golden brown.

The meat is ready when it is so hot that you cannot touch it with your fingers. That is approximately 30 minutes per side. Baste again and sprinkle with Rendezvous world famous seasoning and you are ready to serve.

Yield: 4 servings

Source: Nick Vergos of Charlie Vergos' Rendezvous Restaurant, Memphis, Tennessee by way of www.all-restaurantrecipes.com

"People call it rub—we don't call it rub—it's our seasoning," explains John. "Customers always use the expression 'dry ribs' but we never call our ribs that. When I hear that, I think of beef jerky! You can go as far back in history as you want and you will never, ever see the expression 'dry ribs' until the late '60s or '70s. It was just an attempt by others to try and duplicate what *we* do. I tell people that our ribs are neither 'wet' nor 'dry,' but that they are Rendezvous ribs. And I don't mind telling you that they are juicy!"

I talk with John about the way the ribs are cooked and how some purists insist that charcoal doesn't lend itself to true barbecue. Because the ribs are cooked quickly right over the heat, pundits cry that it's direct grilling, not smoking. John admits that it takes "about two hours" to cook the typical rack, but also argues that there's a lot of smoking going on during that time. When one of the pit crew pries open one of the heavy oven doors, there's smoke in there, and that flavor is permeating the meat.

"Our ribs get the heat from the bed of charcoal and flavor from the smoke," John says. "We baste them with vinegar and put our seasoning on them, and we do have sauce on the side. But you don't want your seasoning or sauce to overpower the meat. You should still be able to taste the meat . . . and the smoke. Some places spend so much time worrying about the sauce—and the sauce is so overwhelming—that you might as well put the sauce on bread because that's all you taste. You don't taste the meat."

John also explains that the ribs they use aren't spareribs or baby-back, but loin-back. "We try to buy them at 2¼ pounds or smaller. So in essence, they are baby-back ribs that have grown up," he says with a smile. "Personally, we think that it's the best cut of ribs, and so do a lot of our customers." He must be right: according to his own records, about 3,600 customers come here to eat ribs on a typical Saturday night.

When it comes to mouth-watering pie, Corky's pecan variety is at the zenith. For the first 10 years, it was made by Corky's president Barry Pelts' mom and aunt. At one point, the pie-making operation got so big that they needed a 10,000-square-foot plant, so they handed off the recipe to a local company that now makes them. ©2008 Michael Karl Witzel

Years ago, the original Rendezvous could only seat 80. Today, the colossal dining room can pack in 750 rib lovers. "What really put us on the map and boosted the Rendezvous reputation is that Kemmons Wilson—the original founder of the Holiday Inns—came here during the early 1960s," recalls John. "Of course, he ate some ribs and loved them. He also fell in love with the place. So, whenever a franchisee would come into Memphis, Wilson would bring them to the Rendezvous.

"In the years that followed, the people who came to town while on their way to open a Holiday Inn franchise in Atlanta or Nashville would try our ribs and find out for themselves just what Wilson was talking about. When they returned home, they would tell their friends that 'When you go to Memphis, be sure to go across the street from the Peabody to the basement restaurant in the alley . . . there is a wonderful rib place there.'"

But the story of the Rendezvous is about more than just word-of-mouth. It's a true American success story, one that began during the 1900s, when Vergos' grandfather—also named John—emigrated from Greece with his family. He tried his luck at a number of odd jobs but eventually ended up in Memphis, where he broke into the fast food business before it was known as such. "My grandfather opened a diner and was the first person to sell foot-long hot dogs for a nickel on Beale Street," says John.

When he was old enough, Vergos' son Charlie followed him down the restaurant path and eventually opened a hash house of his own. He called it Wimpy's (like the hamburger-loving character of Popeye cartoon fame) and went in partners with his brother-in-law. The pair sold standard diner comfort food like meatloaf and mashed potatoes, hamburgers, sandwiches, and pie.

But according to local lore, things didn't work out so well between the two. Charlie split with his brother-in-law and left him to run Wimpy's, opening a small sandwich shop of his own in the basement. He called the place the Rendezvous Snack Bar and was open only in the evening. Unlike the diner upstairs, his idea was to keep the menu simple—smoke hams and then sell ham sandwiches, along with lots of ice cold beer.

As it turned out, the basement was equipped with an old coal chute, a bricked-in compartment that Charlie cleaned out and converted into a pit. As he had planned, he gave his customers scant choice: ham on rye bread, with or without the cheese, and mustard. Later, he added salami to the menu. If you asked, he would slice up all the ingredients and serve it to you on a platter. The snack bar quickly became a hangout for the men folk of Memphis while their wives were busy doing their shopping chores downtown.

One day Charlie's meat salesman came in with a case of ribs and suggested that Charlie try his hand at cooking them

For those who like their barbecue drenched in sticky sauce, the experience at the Rendezvous may seem a bit foreign. However, one bite will confirm the fact that these racks of pork more than hold their own. This style of cooking is in a class of its own, to be savored on its own merits and not compared with the so-called "wet" variety. As the menu proclaims, "Not since Adam has a rib been this famous." ©2008 Michael Karl Witzel

During the 1930s, Leonard's Pit Barbecue offered food delivery by bicycle and pioneered today's popular take-out and catering services. In the 1940s and 1950s, Leonard's was the world's largest barbecue drive-in restaurant, with 20 carhops serving the daily parade of patrons who parked under the canopies. ©2008 Michael Karl Witzel

Aunt Ruthie's Memphis-style Mustard Slaw

4 pounds white cabbage, finely chopped (preferably in food processor)
1 large green pepper, seeded, stemmed, and very finely minced
1 medium onion, grated
2 medium carrots, peeled, shredded, and finely minced
4 teaspoons celery seed
2 teaspoons salt
1 teaspoon freshly ground black pepper
1 teaspoon freshly ground white pepper
24 ounces French's yellow mustard
1 to 1-1/2 cups granulated sugar
1/4 cup apple cider vinegar
1/4 cup Frank's Red Hot (original) sauce to taste (or smaller amount of Tabasco)

Place chopped cabbage in a large mixing bowl and add the green pepper, onions, and carrots and toss together. In another mixing bowl add mustard and whisk in sugar and vinegar. Add celery seed, black pepper, white pepper and salt to the mustard mixture. At this stage add about half the amount of the hot sauce and whisk together. Pour this dressing over the cabbage mixture and mix until well coated. If needed, add more hot sauce. Serve immediately.

Serves: 12

SOURCE: FROM THE FAMILY RECIPE COLLECTION OF RUTH YOUNG

for a little change of pace. "In those days the loin back ribs that we used were just a byproduct that really were not sold to the public," explains John. "My father started grilling those ribs in the pit, but wasn't really sure how to cook them and how to season them."

It didn't take long for him to hit on a flavorful formula, drawing from the generations of recipes handed down from his Greek lineage. He decided to put together all of the spices that he grew up with—ingredients like oregano, garlic, salt, and pepper—and add chili powder in honor of his dad's spicy short-order fare. As food lore has it, the meat salesmen commented that it "tastes great, but looks awful . . . barbecue should be red." So Charlie added paprika for color and the famous Rendezvous seasoning was born.

Soon, Charlie's meat man was delivering a case of ribs every week. As customers learned of the ribs' mouth-watering

mystique, ham sandwich sales dwindled. The ribs propelled the small basement snack bar to a "rendezvous" with greatness.

Today, to honor family legacy, Charles Vergos' Rendezvous serves the same type of mustard slaw inspired by the elder Vergos' pioneering hot dog days. And, as an homage to father Charlie's early diner—and later snack bar—experiences, the house appetizer is made up of sliced sausage, pickles, and cheddar cheese—all served on a plate. To become a legend, you sometimes have to look to the past.

Everything I have read or heard about the Rendezvous is true. The ribs are in a class by themselves, unique and a true Memphis original. The Vergos family, along with the red seasoning that made it all happen, has left a lasting impression on me. Vergos sends me off fully laden, complete with a bottle of the Rendezvous Famous Barbecue Sauce and my very own shaker of secret seasoning.

Opposite: Rendezvous chef and pitmaster Pat Donohue presents the best of his restaurant for tourists and locals alike: pork ribs seasoned with special spices, baked beans, seasoned rice, rolls, and a glass of Coca-Cola. Visitors are 60 percent local, 40 percent out-of-town. If Memphis residents have guests from out of town, it's tradition to bring them to the Rendezvous for dinner. ©2008 Michael Karl Witzel

Behind the counter at Neely's Interstate, family photos provide a poignant backdrop to a display of miniature pecan pies and other treats designed for to-go orders. ©2008 Michael Karl Witzel

MARLOWE'S RIBS & RESTAURANT, ELVIS PRESLEY BOULEVARD

I forge through the line of people waiting to get into the Rendezvous and return into the hidden alleyways of Memphis on my way to the garage and my old Chevy. Before I can digest my ribs, I'm "motorvatin'" down Elvis Presley Boulevard, headed south on the old U.S. route, through a seedy gauntlet of no-tell motels, abandoned stores, junk-car lots, and other threadbare businesses.

Finally, I hit the more civilized portion of the strip near Whitehaven, an area populated by strip malls and other shops, including all of the city's Elvis Presley museums, hotels, shrines, and attractions. I pull over near the Graceland gates, jump out, and snap a few obligatory pictures.

Just down the road a piece, the sight of a pink Airstream trailer catches my eye. It's painted to look like a pig, complete with hooves, tail, and a snout sticking out in the front. I hit the brakes and as I find a place to park, I encounter the "Hogzilla" van, an early-1970s "short bus" repainted with a crazy cast

of comical swine, including Hogzilla himself. There's even a porcine incarnation of the glitter group KISS, painted above the doors.

I begin to wonder if I'm at the right place, but soon find out that the whimsical props are not the whole story at Marlowe's. The first thing that grabs your attention after you pass through the front door is how seriously they take barbecue. The evidence is right there in your face—the entire vestibule and waiting area is packed with a forest of trophies topped off with golden pigs and other icons—awards won at the "Memphis in May" and other tri-state barbecue competitions.

This afternoon, Marlowe's is gearing up to serve a whole busload of Elvis lovers with that award-winning barbecue, and preparations are in full swing. The tables are set, the pork is cooking, and the ribs are almost ready. Fortunately, there are

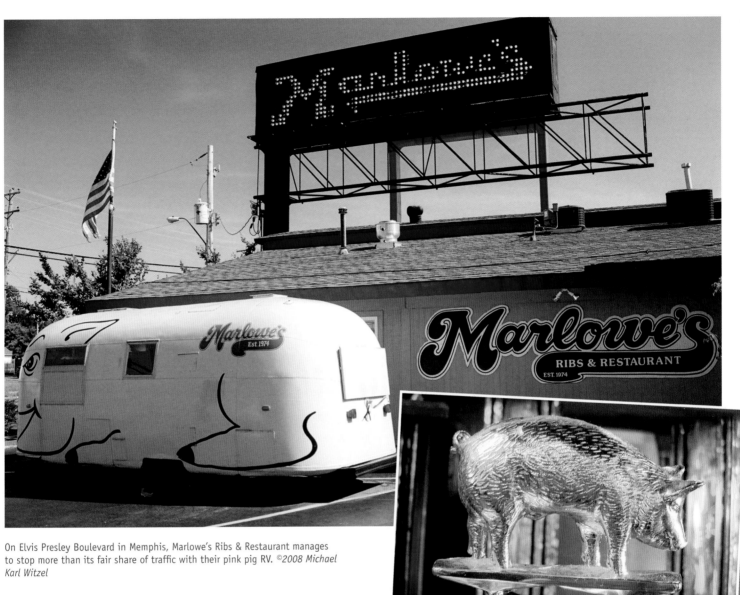

On Elvis Presley Boulevard in Memphis, Marlowe's Ribs & Restaurant manages to stop more than its fair share of traffic with their pink pig RV. ©2008 Michael Karl Witzel

Marlowe's has won many state and regional barbecue competitions and proudly displays their numerous trophies in their front lobby. ©2008 Michael Karl Witzel

a few minutes of free time before the mayhem officially starts, so I sit down to chat with owner Melissa Coleman at one of the many tables layered with vintage Elvis ephemera under glass.

As my eyes peruse the gold records, antique barber's chair, vintage phone booth, and other bric-a-brac that set the Marlowe's mood, I learn that Melissa's father opened the restaurant in 1973. Back then, it was called the White Haven Ranch House and was the place Elvis used to come for what would later be called the "Elvis Burger." Melissa tells me that they had the first salad bar setup in the Whitehaven area and that they served fare such as grilled hamburgers and sliced roast beef. The neighborhood demographic was young and well off . . . and they didn't have tourists for customers.

When Elvis was still alive, the elder Coleman started a chain called Danver's for the Marriott Corporation, a roast beef place

that served sandwiches like Arby's does today, only a lot juicier. They had locations all over the Mid-South and Marlowe's was originally going to be part of that chain. But Coleman had other plans: he decided to get out of the partnership and run the restaurant on his own. In 1982, he changed the name in honor of Melissa's younger sister, Marlowe.

"My dad had a really creative mind when it came to all things relating to restaurants, but he didn't have any barbecue

experience," Melissa admits. To get up to speed in the business, Mr. Coleman hired a man who worked for the local Tops barbecue chain to build him a pit. Another guy trained them how to cook barbecue on it and taught them the various tricks of the trade.

Coleman may have started at a disadvantage when it came to cooking, but in the formative years of the eatery, he more than made up for it with ideas that built up the business on a shoestring budget. His first creation was the "pig bus," the vehicle that I first encountered in the parking lot. Coleman hired artist Ruben Drewery to repaint the van with pig-themed pictures.

The van was the linchpin in his scheme to catch the interest of the people who were staying at the KOA campground near the Elvis mansion. "Once the tourists staying at that camp got [their RVs] hooked up and unpacked, they didn't much feel

Above: On occasion, the serious barbecuer in Memphis will cook a whole hog in a large smoker or barbecue pit, producing a porcine product that looks a lot like this example, captured in all its glory at the yearly "Memphis in May" barbecue competition. ©2008 Michael Karl Witzel

Opposite: Marlowe's Ribs & Restaurant general manager Melissa "Missy" Coleman shows off one of the many trophies her restaurant has won at local and regional barbecue competitions (this one for the Tennessee Funfest). ©2008 Michael Karl Witzel

like going anywhere else. Many didn't have any other form of transportation, either," says Melissa. Her father thought that the funky pig bus would be a great way to bring customers back and forth to Marlowe's for barbecue. "There weren't many restaurants around here back then, but it was a real busy area around the campground. So you can just picture the scene: my dad pulls up with this loud, backfiring bus and starts giving people rides back and forth. They loved it. People were having the time of their life."

Around that time a customer came in and announced that he had an old Cadillac limousine that he wanted to get rid of. The wheels started spinning and Coleman came up with his next big brainstorm: why not paint the limo pink and start picking up customers in style? The idea proved an even bigger hit with the tourists. The pig bus was parked and soon one limo turned into four. Marlowe's had its signature service.

"People do take notice of our pink Cadillacs," Melissa says. "I get calls all the time to reserve them for weddings and for people to be taken to the Elvis Chapel." Coleman noticed that people visiting Memphis from out of town really got a kick out of being picked up at their hotel and taken on a roundtrip to Marlowe's—even if they had their own vehicle. On some nights, virtually all of the

Above: Marlowe's is unique in the fact that it employs its very own fleet of pink Cadillac limousines. Free of charge, they pick up and drop off customers at their hotel rooms in Memphis, taking them to and from Marlowe's to dine. ©2008 Michael Karl Witzel

Right: In the kitchen of Marlowe's, Edward Wicks applies the finishing touches to platters of barbecue as main entrées are paired with various side orders. ©2008 Michael Karl Witzel

guests at Marlowe's arrive by way of the limousines.

It's a great setup. The limo drivers get immediate feedback about how the customers liked their meal and the service. On occasion, Melissa's father just so happens to be one of the restaurant's drivers. "My father's favorite job at Marlowe's is limousine driver. When we started out with them, he was the first official limousine driver that we had."

Coleman's father is also responsible for the barbecue cooker that's smack dab in the center of Marlowe's where the customers can see it. The one-of-a-kind cooker is enclosed inside a room with glass windows so that people sitting at their tables can get a first-hand look at the process. When the door or pass-through window opens, the wonderful aroma of smoked ribs and pork shoulder permeates the room.

The stainless-steel smoker was built without any directions, its design and construction aided by a pair of friends who were specialists in other areas, like steel fabrication and smoker design. Inside, the cooker features an electric rotisserie that rotates the meat throughout the heat and a special firebox to the side where various types of wood can be placed to add the smoke flavor. The dials and controls are all custom made and lack any sort of labeling, adding to its mystique.

Above: Pulled pork is a Memphis tradition and is served at most barbecue joints in town, including Marlowe's. This succulent example was cooked up by the Pork Me Tender crew at the annual Memphis in May competition and is the standard that many of the restaurants strive for. ©2008 Michael Karl Witzel

Right: Server Michelle Ramos presents platter after platter of food to a receptive audience. Here, pulled-pork platters, complete with a baked potato and green beans, are on their way to the tables. ©2008 Michael Karl Witzel

Awaiting a bus of senior citizens out to see Graceland and taste some Memphis barbecue, Marlowe's prepares long tables in preparation for the crowd. ©2008 Michael Karl Witzel

Chris Nielson showcases the specialty that draws the crowds to Marlowe's: barbecued pork ribs. Cooked in a special smoker situated in the center of the dining room, they are a crowd-pleaser.
©2008 Michael Karl Witzel

Marlowe's manager, Chris Nielson, is busy loading the cooker. In the small prep area opposite the oven door he unwraps pork shoulders and sprinkles them with seasoning, rubbing the spices around the periphery of the meat. Simultaneously, racks of ribs are on their way to being done. He takes one out and mops it with a generous dollop of barbecue sauce, preparing it for a customer.

He shows me the firebox where a glowing blue gas flame enters from a large pipe, firing the wood that's placed inside. "We use hickory, but sometimes we add some apple or other types of wood according to the season," Chris tells me. "We have a lot of tour buses come in with big parties, so it's a lot of work getting all of the food ready for them when they come in. We do barbecue pizza, pulled pork

Because of Marlowe's close proximity to Graceland, it hosts a high volume of Elvis fans on a daily basis. On the premises, diners may visit Marlowe's gift shop and manager J. J. Grady, stocked to the rafters with all kinds of Elvis memorabilia and trinkets, including key chains, hats, T-shirts, postcards, and more. ©2008 Michael Karl Witzel

Ribs, chicken, baked potato, and iced tea—an unbeatable foursome and a favorite combination at Marlowe's. ©2008 Michael Karl Witzel

sandwiches, spaghetti . . . but mostly we do ribs, about a thousand pounds every week."

By this time, the activities inside Marlowe's are picking up. Melissa has excused herself to take care of her duties in the rear kitchen, while Chris does triple duty as pitmaster, waiter, and entertainer. As the first wave of oldsters pour in and take their seats at preset dining tables, he moves quickly back and forth from the oven to deliver plates of ribs and side orders, all while keeping the people jumping with his banter.

Chris takes the time to serve up a generous portion to me as well, and I retreat to a corner near the Elvis souvenir shop (yes, Marlowe's has one on the premises) with my own platter. The ribs are quite tasty, along with the assortment of standard barbecue side dishes. As I pour on the sauce and reduce my rack to stripped bones, I study the racks of T-shirts, key chains, and other ephemera and think about

At Tops, they cook from 1,200 to 1,500 pork shoulders in a single week, outpacing all other restaurants in the Memphis area. To ensure consistent quality control across all locations, each restaurant employs a "master cook" trained in all aspects of pit cooking and circumventing the various problems that may arise.
©2008 Michael Karl Witzel

Wildhorse Saloon Pulled Pork

Step One: BBQ Rib Rub
2 cups granulated sugar
3/4 cup chili powder
4 tablespoons onion powder
6 tablespoons paprika
3 tablespoons cumin
1/4 cup salt
3 tablespoons black pepper
1 tablespoon garlic powder
1 tablespoon cayenne pepper
4 tablespoons plus 2 teaspoons seasoning salt
Combine all ingredients and whisk together well with a wire whisk and set aside

Step Two: Pulled Pork
1 (10-pound) Boston pork butt
1 cup Rib Rub recipe (above)

Season pork with rib rub and let sit in refrigerator for a minimum of 4 hours. Place pork in smoker that is between 225 and 250 degrees. Let pork smoke for 6 hours at that temperature. Wrap pork in aluminum foil and continue to smoke for 6 hours more until bone pulls clean.
Chill until warm. Pull into strips and refrigerate. Re-heat pork with Wildhorse Barbecue Sauce (or Memphis-style barbecue sauce) over medium heat until hot.

Source: The Wildhorse Saloon, by way of www.all-restaurantrecipes.com

Inside the dining room of Jim Neely's Interstate Bar-B-Que one can find the "Wall of Fame," a collection of publicity stills showing the celebrities and other notables who have stopped by for a bite to eat. ©2008 Michael Karl Witzel

how back in the day Elvis might have chowed down on some of these ribs in the Jungle Room.

Sure, the atmosphere may be a little kitschy and touristy, but the people who come here are all having a great time, enjoying some of the best ribs this side of Graceland. Everyone needs some kind of escape from reality every now and then, and Marlowe's provides the perfect means for that escape—Elvis style.

I nod to Chris and give him a thumbs-up. He's too busy juggling plates of ribs and pitchers of iced tea to say goodbye.

Leonard Heuberger's logo was a pig in top hat and tails, captioned with the phrase "Mr. Brown Goes to Town." As it cooks, the outside of the meat gets dark and chewy—the part of the cut known by cognoscenti as "Mr. Brown." Meanwhile, the interior, soft but not as deeply flavored, is known as "Miss White." Accordingly, if Mr. Brown goes to town, your chopped-meat sandwich is imbued with plenty of outside morsels of flavor-tinged meat. ©2008 Michael Karl Witzel

I won't soon forget Marlowe's, dedicated in its approach to barbecue and unique in its own right. I say goodbye to Hogzilla, *au revoir* to the pink pig trailer, and so long to the pink stretch limousines.

Neely's Bar-B-Que Restaurant Wet BBQ Ribs

32 ounces ketchup
16 ounces water
6 ounces brown sugar
6 ounces granulated sugar
1 tablespoon black pepper
1 tablespoon onion powder
1 tablespoon ground mustard
2 ounces Neely's Seasoning
2 ounces lemon juice
2 ounces Worcestershire sauce
8 ounces apple cider vinegar
2 ounces corn syrup
3–4 pounds spare ribs

Neely's Seasoning
Mix the following ingredients:

4 ounces paprika
2 ounces granulated sugar
1 teaspoon onion powder

Combine sauce ingredients in a stockpot. Cook at a high temperature and bring to a boil and stir to prevent sticking. Lower temperature and simmer without cover for at least 30 minutes.

Trim a 3- to 4-pound spare rib (remove the upper brisket bone and any other excess; this will produce a St. Louis style rib). Rinse and season rib with Neely's Seasoning, then refrigerate for 4–12 hours.

We recommend that ribs are cooked on an indirect barbecue pit to prevent burning. The ideal temperature is 250 degrees for the first three hours, and 300 degrees for the final three hours.

Load ribs curl side up, so the juices will maintain their moisture. After three hours, turn ribs and increase temperature. Baste ribs with Neely's barbecue sauce during the last 30 minutes of cooking so sauce will not burn.

SOURCE: PATRICK NEELY, NEELY'S BAR-B-QUE RESTAURANT, MEMPHIS, TENNESSEE

Dusk is here and once again, I'm on the road, driving north on Elvis Presley Boulevard. As I pick up speed and try to beat the lights, I glance once more at the Graceland estate and think to myself how small it looks. I pass the Heartbreak Hotel and should be thinking of Elvis, but all I can do is worry about how heartbroken I'll be when I'm a few hundred miles out of Memphis and get a craving for a pulled-pork sandwich with coleslaw.

Elvis was a pretty good performer, I'll grant you that—but his appeal is nowhere near as big as the crowd-pleaser that Memphians know and love as barbecue. Indeed, in my opinion, barbecued pork is the jewel in the crown that elevates Memphis to a place of eminence.

The barbecue that I've sampled here and the hospitability that I've encountered has given me a new appreciation for southern food. To my amazement, I'm even beginning to question my allegiance to Texas brisket. In this town, you can slurp up a plate of barbecue spaghetti any time you want. You can wolf down a pulled-pork sandwich that humiliates everything else that's served between two slices of bread. You can dine on pork ribs prepared with so-called "dry rub" seasoning and discover

that they are as moist and delicious as those suffocated in a thick glaze of barbecue sauce.

When visiting Memphis, the thrill is definitely not gone when it comes to searching for barbecue joints and eating in them. I'm under the spell of this town and its porcine delights and will return here time and time again to eat hearty on the banks of the old Mississippi.

But for now, I have one final barbecue region to explore, so many miles to keep, and so much more barbecue to eat.

Darrell Buchanan mans the counter at the second Payne's Bar-BQ location on Elvis Presley Boulevard in Memphis. Started in 1972 by Horton Payne because "he just wanted to do something on his own," the chain of two eateries is currently run by his widow, Flora. ©2008 Michael Karl Witzel

My stomach is full and my appetite is satisfied, but as the saying goes, "Tomorrow is another day . . . to eat barbecue." So fire up the pits and throw on a whole hog! Next stop, North Carolina—a place that claims to be nothing less than "the cradle of 'cue."

Not to be outdone by the surrounding fast food joints in East Memphis, Corky's Poplar Avenue location features a drive-thru window. Here, Ella Hope greets the next car in line. ©2008 Michael Karl Witzel

Elvis Presley Ate Here

Memphis, Tennessee, is regarded by foodies as the nexus of the barbecue world. To music fans, it's the cradle of rock 'n' roll. There lies Graceland, the humble home of Elvis Aaron Presley, recording star, seller of over one billion records, and connoisseur of barbecue.

Of course, everyone who knows their Elvis trivia is quick to tell you that the King loved his fried peanut-butter-and-banana sandwiches. But Memphians in the know will also inform you that he also had a Cadillac-sized appetite for barbecue sandwiches and the occasional barbecue pizza.

These days, both Elvis and barbecue are big business for Memphis, vying for their share of the tourist's dollar. According to Graceland estimates, some 600,000 visitors a year rock 'n' roll their way through the Presley estate, many forking over $25 for the "platinum tour" of the white-columned abode where he lived, made music, and died.

Unfortunately, you won't see any bronzed racks of baby-back ribs on this tour. What you will learn is that Elvis' father, Vernon, smoked meats in a small room right next to the garage. But it was only temporary: eventually, Elvis converted the ad hoc smokehouse into a shooting range. Afterward, he relied on the local 'cue joints to satisfy his cravings for comfort food take-out.

And for that, he had a big selection. Like so many flamboyant Elvis imitators, Memphis is home to a rabble of local barbecue joints that all claim the King of Rock 'n' Roll either dined there or had their take-out.

"The saying 'Elvis Presley Ate Here' is the cultural equivalent of 'George Washington Slept Here,'" says Robert Thompson, professor of media and culture at Syracuse University. "Every time a place makes a claim that Elvis ate there, it becomes a memorial to his memory, to his life, and to his legend."

And that's precisely what happened to Marlowe's, a Memphis eatery that's been family-owned and operated since 1973. Serving up world-class barbecue along with an eclectic collection of Elvis memorabilia, Marlowe's offers free rides from Graceland-area hotels in their very own Pink limousine. Their claim to fame is the one-of-a-kind "Elvis Burger," the only ground beef sandwich that's sanctioned by Elvis Presley Enterprises.

Touted as "The Burger for the King Himself," it features all of the toppings in which Elvis was known to indulge, including lettuce, tomato, onion, pickles, bacon, cheddar cheese, and savory ham—cut directly from hogs that are smoked on the premises.

"That's why the Elvis Presley estate was kind enough to allow us to name the hamburger after him," explains Melissa Coleman, Marlowe's proprietor. Back during the 1970s, when our place was still called the White Haven Ranch House, it was something that Elvis chose, and he chose to eat here a lot."

Graceland Wall graffiti, Memphis, Tennessee. ©2008 Michael Karl Witzel

Memphis Barbecue Mecca
Corky's Bar-B-Q

5259 Poplar Avenue
Memphis, Tennessee 38119
(901) 685-9744

Welcome to Corky's, home of the Corky's Memphis Brew. The neon-glow Corky's sign with the beer bottle says it all—'50s music blasting from the jukebox, photos plastered all over wood-paneled walls, oil-cloth-covered tables—this is the definitive joint. Once you get past the "joint" feel of the place, leave all your notions behind because Corky's serves up with a style that would make any "classy" restaurant blush with shame.

What started as a family business in 1984 has now become a family extravaganza. Founded by restaurateur Donald Pelts, this Memphis hot spot continues to serve in the style and tradition that he first envisioned. Corky's has it all—pork, brisket, or chicken, each dish is better than the next. These folks know how to plate-up with razzmatazz, flourishing touches created as a feast for the eyes as well as the palate.

Here you can get the best pulled-pork sandwich in town, topped with a generous mound of coleslaw, fabulous slow-cooked ribs that ooze with taste, and a barbecue chicken that holds its tenderness all the way through.

Save your appetite for the sides. Here comes one of the best-looking jumbo baked potatoes, loaded with any kind of meat that you want, plus sour cream, butter, and a generous helping of cheddar cheese. And just in case you've forgotten where you are, the Corky's name is written along the edge of the plate in cursive barbecue sauce lettering. And speaking of barbecue: try those barbecue baked beans served in their own bowl and you will actually float right off your seat with sheer joy.

Just when you thought it couldn't get any better, along comes dessert: banana pudding topped with mounds of whipped cream and a garnish of maraschino; pecan pie drizzled with butterscotch, chocolate, and vanilla sauces; and a cinnamon-dappled peach cobbler accompanied by a dollop of vanilla ice cream. It's a nonstop parade of wonders, served up with a smile by Corky's fantastic wait staff.

(continue overleaf)

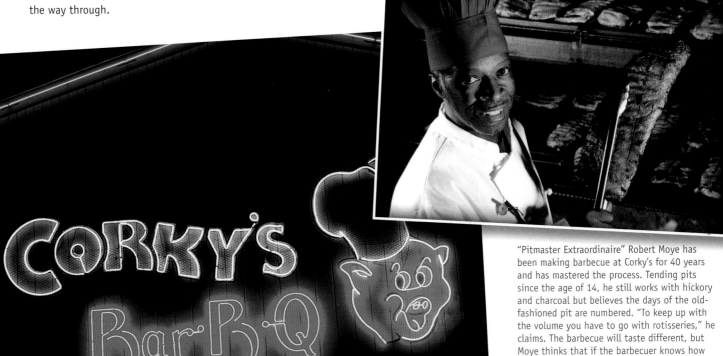

"Pitmaster Extraordinaire" Robert Moye has been making barbecue at Corky's for 40 years and has mastered the process. Tending pits since the age of 14, he still works with hickory and charcoal but believes the days of the old-fashioned pit are numbered. "To keep up with the volume you have to go with rotisseries," he claims. The barbecue will taste different, but Moye thinks that if the barbecuer knows how to compensate with seasonings, the customer won't complain. *Courtesy of Corky's Bar-B-Q*

According to *Memphis Magazine*, Corky's BBQ has been voted the number-one barbecue in Memphis for 14 straight years. Corky's has been featured in *USA Today*, *The New York Times*, *The Wall Street Journal*, and *Bon Appetit* magazine. Located on the busy Poplar Avenue in Memphis, its glowing neon and happy-faced pig chef greet customers. ©2008 Michael Karl Witzel

Above: At Corky's BBQ, the interior dining area is decidedly relaxed and a Southern "roadhouse" in its look and feel—the perfect place to eat with your hands along with a stack of fresh napkins. ©2008 Michael Karl Witzel

Right: Lyntoy Brandon displays a freshly baked apple cobbler in the kitchen of Corky's BBQ. Unlike some of the bare-bones barbecue joints of the South that sometime skimp on sweet treats, the desserts are numerous at Corky's, including chocolate fudge pie with ice cream, pecan pie, bread pudding pie, banana pudding, root beer floats, and ice cream. ©2008 Michael Karl Witzel

Back in the early 1970s, Donald Pelts quit the family furniture business and opened his first restaurant in the midtown area of Memphis. The place was hopping, but by the 1980s Pelts wanted to bring his idea of world-class, authentic barbecue to Memphis. He took his idea into East Memphis, an area of town where hospitals, office buildings, and residences flourished.

As Barry Pelts, Donald's son, explains, "He wanted to open up a real joint, meaning he wanted the '50s music, the old barn wood, and waiters in black bowties and white jackets. To do something no one else had done—that is dine-in seating with waiters and all, but also having a drop-through window that puts out food faster than a McDonald's. And that is a concept that no one had done anywhere else in America: you were either fast food or you were casual dining."

As everyone will tell you the key to success is location, location, location. And Donald Pelts was willing to wait four years for the perfect spot. When it showed up in the form of a failed barbecue restaurant at 5259 Poplar Avenue, naysayers told him he was crazy for thinking he could succeed where another had failed. His reply was simple: "I'm going to get the best location, I'm going to bring in the best management, I'm going to make the best quality ribs. I am not going to skimp anywhere and if it fails I'll know I failed with all my guns fully loaded."

As if to prove the doomsayers wrong, Corky's grew at an astonishing rate in its first 10 years. Everybody but Donald was surprised by the restaurant's success. When asked what the keys to their good fortune are, both he and son Barry emphatically state that they're good management and excellent personnel.

Corky's staff longevity is proof positive that every element of the restaurant business is important to the Pelts. As Barry states, "We have well-paid people here and well-paid managers . . . we are extremely management-intensive. All our kitchen managers started with us by 1980. Our average employee has been with us probably 18 years. I've got three busboys that started with my dad in 1972, so you are talking 35 years. In the restaurant business, turnover is usually about every nine months."

What draws the 1,200 plus customers in each day? According to Barry, "Without doubt it is the consistency. They know every single day what they are going to get . . . and it's our servers. Most of our servers have been with us 15 to 20 years. They make it a fun experience. It's not just coming into the restaurant, getting served your food, wolfing it down, and then you're gone. Our servers make it a fun experience."

According to pitmaster Robert Moye, it's the ribs. Corky's serves the best St. Louis–cut pork sparerib, hand-trimmed and slow-cooked over a combination of charcoal and hickory for 6 to 7 hours. And they are served two ways: wet or dry. Moye first met Donald Pelts back in the 1970s when Donald owned his mid-town restaurant. Today, Moye is Corky's spokesperson on the QVC channel, his image graces the cover of their menu, and he even appears in local Corky's commercials.

Still, others might think the key to Corky's success is their award-winning sauce, created 25 years ago by the Pelts. Corky's Original BBQ Sauce has been cited as the number-one retail sauce in America by *Southern Living* magazine, and it has won the *Good Housekeeping* Institute Award.

Yet, as Barry states, "The bottom line is that you can have all the great sauces in the world but if you don't execute it, if you don't give people a good experience, if the food is not consistently good, if the service isn't good, if the bathrooms aren't clean . . . we are all about things being right. If you go in and buy the best raw products, you take your time and cook it right, and you execute every day, your likelihood of success is good."A

Left: Upon being presented this pulled-pork sandwich at Corky's, my first thought and comment was "How do you eat this thing?" My answer came quickly from waitress Anita Patrick: "You have to mash it down with your hand first. Then you eat it just like you would any other sandwich or hamburger. Two hands and plenty of napkins!" **Above:** Corky's BBQ serves up a baked potato that is a meal in itself, if not a work of culinary artistry.
Below right: The cultivation, preparation, and consumption of beans are recorded in the tombs of ancient Egypt and in the Old Testament. In some Eastern cultures, legumes were a basic dietary staple that can be traced back more than 20,000 years. Corky's BBQ beans are a much more recent creation, but are nonetheless a must-have when dining on barbecue in Memphis.
Below left: In Memphis, Corky's BBQ has pork ribs down to a science. Seared with crosscut grill marks, they are slow-cooked over charcoal and basted with Memphis-style sauce. Just slather on a little bit more from the bottle and enjoy. Swallow then repeat. All ©2008 Michael Karl Witzel

CHAPTER 4

North Carolina

PERFECTING THE ART OF PIG PICKIN'

Southern Barbecue.

LEAVING THE TRIANGLE OF RALEIGH, DURHAM, AND CHAPEL HILL, I'm traveling Southeast on Highway 70 in a beat-up, 1953 Chevrolet pickup truck with my windows rolled down, earbuds in, and my iPod set to shuffle. Like a ghost, I slip through towns like Clayton, Wilsons Mills, Selma, and Princeton, witnessing a region struggling to bridge the divide to the high-tech industries of tomorrow while still clinging to the timeworn traditions of the past. This is tobacco farming country and North Carolina is still the nation's leading producer.

About 45 miles out of Goldsboro, I can't help but notice a certain odiferous "fragrance" hanging in the air and permeating my nostrils, but I know it's not the smell of tobacco fields. A few moments later, I come upon a large billboard and suddenly understand where the pungent aroma is coming from: "Nahunta Pork Center, Turn Left Five Miles."

"Well, help my time," as they say in this neck of the woods—I'm deep in the heart of pork country, where raising hogs is second only to tobacco.

A few miles down the road, I jog left on NC-581 and make a quick detour to the town of Nahunta, curious to see what this spectacle is all about. Of course, I've never seen anything like it. Texas doesn't have them. Memphis doesn't have them. Kansas City doesn't have them. This place is a megastore for everything pig. When in North Carolina, you don't go to a Piggly Wiggly to pick up your pork. Here, only a pork center will do.

Known as the "Pork King," Nahunta Pork Center is the largest "all-pork" retail displayer in the eastern United States. This place has it all, including whole hogs for barbecuing, sausages, country-cured hams, shoulders, and sides. They even

All of the pit-cooking restaurants in Lexington have a connection to a man by the name of Warner Stamey. Stamey learned the craft from Jesse Swicegood. Swicegood and Sid Weaver are the two gentlemen credited for the origin of "Lexington-style" barbecue. At the Bar-B-Q Center, chef John Tetter chops pork by hand, the same way they have been doing it for generations. ©2008 Michael Karl Witzel

Opposite: A sliced pork platter takes center stage at Bridges Barbecue Lodge. Served with fries, red coleslaw, pickles, and a tomato slice, it's a hands-down favorite for Shelby locals. Frank's RedHot Original Cayenne Pepper Sauce is made with a premium blend of aged cayenne peppers and was the secret ingredient used in the first ever Buffalo wing in Buffalo, New York, in 1964. ©2008 Michael Karl Witzel

Above: A Little Pigs of America Barbecue sign advertises genuine hickory-smoked barbecue, somewhere along the roadside in Asheville, North Carolina. ©2008 Michael Karl Witzel

Left: Little Pigs of America was one of the earliest barbecue chains in the United States. Based in Memphis, it boasted numerous locations throughout the South. In early 1965, Little Pigs filed for bankruptcy; however, a number of locations still remain.
©2008 Michael Karl Witzel

sell fully cooked products like barbecued spareribs, smoked loin roast, and pork chops. Consider the wonder of it all: when was the last time that you could pick up your liver pudding, chitterlings, and souse all at one store?

Frankly, I must admit that souse—pork trimmings that are chopped, pickled, seasoned, and jelled—is one commodity that will most likely never find its way to my dining room table. Nevertheless, it's a potent reminder that the pig reigns supreme in North Carolina and that nothing from the animal goes to waste.

This philosophy of food frugality has been practiced since the days when Sir Walter Raleigh first tried to establish a settlement here and later, when settlers from the Virginia colony built their outpost in the region. In those days, swine were often released into the wild to forage. When the time came to eat, would-be diners hunted them down. Once the animal was shot, it was promptly butchered, dressed, and barbecued.

At the Bar-B-Q Center in Lexington, you can still get old-fashioned, pit-cooked barbecue served to you in your car. ©2008 Michael Karl Witzel

Today, the Bridges family continues the traditions begun by Red Bridges at the Bridges Barbecue Lodge in Shelby. From right to left: Debbie Bridges-Webb, son Chase Ramsey, grandson Parker Ramsey, and daughter Natalie Ramsey. ©2008 Michael Karl Witzel

The resulting bounty created a social event known to North Carolinians as a "pig pickin'"—a large outdoor picnic focused on the hog roast. The ritual began as the carcass was prepared for the pit, which in days of old was simply a hole dug into the ground and filled with hot coals. The pig was suspended over the heat by means of a metal grate or other support. Since the cooking was slow, it provided ample time for revelers to party all night while they "watched the pig." Men folk consumed copious amounts of drink and told tall tales, as women prepared the side dishes that were traditionally served with the pork.

Today, the grand pig pickin's of yesterday are fewer and far between. Hogs don't run wild in the greenbelts of suburbia and there are ordinances against building open fires. Now, the time-harried settlers of America's bedroom communities hunt down their food in the grocery aisles, skin the cardboard, and kill the taste with microwaves.

Fortunately, the hand-me-down barbecue traditions of the Old North State have been kept alive by a number of stalwarts who refuse to allow the art form to expire. From the east to the west and the Piedmont to the plains, the card-carrying members of the "wood-fired" guild ply their smoky trade in public restaurants that are open to all. In spite of spiraling insurance, the rising tide of chain restaurants, and new regulations that threaten to put them out of business, they thrive.

Unused for the moment, the wooden chopping block at Lexington's Bar-B-Q Center stands dormant, awaiting the next frenzied round of pork-chopping activity. ©2008 Michael Karl Witzel

Gene Medlin and his wife Linda are perhaps the most congenial barbecue couple in the state of North Carolina. Their Carolina Bar-B-Q restaurant is the epitome of Southern hospitality, serving with a friendly smile the full bounty of western North Carolina barbecue. ©2008 Michael Karl Witzel

At Carolina Bar-B-Q, the hush puppies are as big as meatballs and worth the trip to Statesville alone. Where did the funny name originate? Some say from Confederate soldiers who sat beside a campfire preparing their meals. When they heard Yankee soldiers coming, they tossed their yapping dogs some of the fried cornmeal cakes with the command "Hush, puppies!" ©2008 Michael Karl Witzel

WILBER'S BARBECUE, GOLDSBORO One such establishment is Wilber's Barbecue, one of the legendary pits of this region that still utilizes real wood to cook its barbecue. Wilber's is one of those fortunate roadside joints with a superb location, anchored on the side of Highway 70 in Goldsboro. When customers whizzing by in their cars see the red-brick, colonial-style building with its white window trim and red-and-yellow sign, they need not travel any farther for food.

But don't expect any fancy variations of the word barbecue here. In North Carolina, you will quickly discover that most barbecue joints don't care to use the cute word-and-letter combinations that some of the other three regions do (of course, there are always exceptions). The barbecue here—and the eateries that serve it—are honest, with no need to cloak the identity of their product in some clever title.

Inside, I'm told by the waitress that Wilbur Shirley is around back by the pits, getting one of his mobile catering rigs ready to deliver a load of barbecue to a local sporting event. I spirit myself around to the back of the building and follow my nose to the pits, where I meet up with Wilber and his small cadre of helpers. He greets me in typical North Carolina fashion, friendly and welcoming. It's great to be in the South.

As he finishes up his task, he tells me that he got his start "right here in North Carolina." He was a country boy who just sort of fell into it. "I went to town to start to work and got on at Griffin's Barbecue," he says. "I went to work for him when I was about 20 years old and then I went to Korea for two years." He continued working at Griffin's upon his return. "I got a pretty good idea of everything that was involved. I ran the place and managed the hiring, the firing, the cooking, the selling—the whole nine yards."

Wilber's Barbecue is located along a busy stretch of Highway 70, just outside of Goldsboro, North Carolina. About 100 miles from the Atlantic Ocean, it's a popular stop for tourists and truckers passing through. The close proximity of the Seymour Johnson Air Force Base ensures a steady stream of barbecue lovers as well. ©2008 Michael Karl Witzel

After 13 years as an apprentice, Shirley decided that it was time to get after it for himself. The building that he owns today was up for sale and he was interested. The owner just had a heart attack and was planning to close it. "I just had a desire to have a place of my own and I got it," he states. "Then you get so poor that you can't get out and then you get so poor that you can't stay, so you just keep on going." It must be true, since Wilber's has been open for 45 years.

Shirley also clues me in to the fact that the barbecue at Wilber's is eastern North Carolina style. That means that the meat prepared here is plain, whole-hog pork. After it's cooked, the meat is chopped up by hand until it's the consistency of a fine mince. No special preparations are made to the meat

U.S. 64 on the Yadkin River between 1000 Trails Campground and Lexington. The origin of the Tarheel nickname is mysterious, although most historians agree that the moniker derives from North Carolina's long history as a producer of naval stores—tar, pitch, rosin, and turpentine—all of which were culled from the State's extensive pine forests. ©2008 Michael Karl Witzel

Wilber Shirley is the owner and operator of Wilber's Barbecue in Goldsboro, North Carolina. "I think the whole-pig method is the real key that makes ours a little different from a lot of places," he says. "We cook it on the wood and get a flavor from the smoke, and then we try to cook it to where it's not so greasy . . . because we found out that people this day and time are conscious about their cholesterol." ©2008 Michael Karl Witzel

Left: At Wilber's, Eddie Radford demonstrates how the pits are covered during the cooking process. Inside, whole hogs are supported by thick metal poles over the coals. When the embers die down, fresh charcoal is added from the woodpile with a shovel until the cooking process is completed. It's a labor- and time-intensive process that few places wish to undertake. Retired principal Eddie Radford is Wilber Shirley's right-hand man. No longer watching over the welfare of students, he makes sure that the pits are running smoothly and that the customers are fed. In North Carolina, where pork barbecue is king, it's an equally important occupation. ©2008 Michael Karl Witzel

Right: To alleviate rising insurance costs, Wilber's built a detached pit behind the restaurant. Made of cinder block and metal sheeting, it can be easily replaced if a fire occurs—something that happens every so often during the process of barbecuing whole hog over burning embers. ©2008 Michael Karl Witzel

Opposite: Clarence Lewis is responsible for the barbecue pits at Wilber's Barbecue in Goldsboro. His job is to keep the woodpile stoked with fresh logs. After the wood burns down, he loads the hot charcoal into a wheelbarrow with a shovel, and then distributes it in the pits, where it is needed. ©2008 Michael Karl Witzel

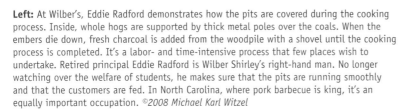

before cooking, either. The quality and grade of the meat, how it's butchered, and the patient, slow-cooking process, are what make the pork so appetizing. Of course, there are numerous tricks and techniques that have to be followed along the way to get it just right.

Unlike some of the cooking setups in Texas and Kansas City, Wilber's barbecue pits are located in an outbuilding in the back of the main restaurant. The cinder-block structure has a walkway down the center, with waist-high pits situated on each side. Metal rods hold the hogs in place over the smoldering coals. The pits also have metal covers that are closed when the pork is cooking. Wilber explains the reasoning behind the shack's expendable nature: "We have burn-ups here once in a while and that's just part of the game, but we don't have insurance coverage on that building because it would make the insurance for the restaurant too high."

Wilber's right-hand man is Eddie Radford, a retired professor and school principal. He points out a modest pile of burning logs in a small depression dug into the ground just to the left of the pit shack. Another man—Clarence Lewis— shuttles between a mountain of split hickory wood and the fire, adding logs and kindling with a large pitchfork. It's hot and backbreaking work, with only a wooden chair provided for breaks. Ward points out that "as the wood burns down, the coals are moved inside the pit with a wheelbarrow."

We go inside and Radford leads me through the smoky inner sanctum of Wilber's barbecue, lifting up one of the metal lids to showcase the whole hog that's cooking inside. The interior air is depleted with smoke and I try to catch my breath without coughing, like a teenager who has just tried his first cigarette. "We put the hogs on at night and then finish them up during the wee hours for early in the morning," Radford

explains. "Usually, you should be able to cook them in eight hours before they are cooked and ready to be chopped."

We meet Wilber on the opposite end of the pit and he reveals one of his cooking secrets. "With our method of cooking, we put the rib side of the meat down," he reveals. "Our heat rises up from the coals at the bottom of the pit and then the juice from the meat drips back onto those hot coals. That's where you get the good flavor.

"We used to season the hog when we turned it over, but it was too messy," he continues. "We start it with the rib side down and then we turn it over when it is almost done, by a couple of three times, on the skin side. Now, we season it lightly when we chop it, because you can add but you can't take away. We sprinkle salt and pepper on it as we season it . . . and then we pour on a special vinegar-base sauce or kitchen dip that we make."

When it comes to customers adding even more barbecue sauce in the dining room, Wilber provides them with bottles of a ruddy concoction he calls "Wilber's Barbecue Sauce," a homemade recipe that he also sells. "It's Spicy Good," claims

In North Carolina, there are two regional traditions for pork: in the eastern part of the state, the preference is to cook the whole hog, as is done at Wilber's Barbecue in Goldsboro (cut in halves). Here, the dominant sauce ingredients are vinegar and hot peppers. From the Piedmont westward, the norm is Lexington-style barbecue, which defers to pork shoulder served with a thin vinegar- or tomato-based sauce that some refer to as "dip." ©2008 Michael Karl Witzel

Eastern-style North Carolina Sauce

1 cup apple cider vinegar
1 teaspoon crushed red pepper
1 teaspoon salt
1/4 teaspoon pepper

Place in a bottle and shake up real good. If you desire some extra "zing," add a dash or two of Texas Pete hot sauce.

SOURCE: ADAPTED FROM A RECIPE USED AT PARKER'S BARBECUE RESTAURANT, WILSON, NORTH CAROLINA

Right: While those to the east of the North Carolina dividing line swear by the thin, watery sauce that they use to enhance their pork, those in the western part of the state see nothing wrong with adding tomato products to their sauce. Some say that they also have been known to add pretty much anything else that is edible, as long as the result tastes good. At Parker's Barbecue in Wilson, the thin, clear variation rules the roost. ©2008 Michael Karl Witzel

Below: Traditionally, cracklings (or cracklins) are slow-roasted on the barbecue or deep fried in lard. At Bridges Barbecue Lodge in Shelby, it's not unusual to see customers request pieces of this crispy, crunchy pig skin over everything else, where they are promptly dipped in sauce and eaten. ©2008 Michael Karl Witzel

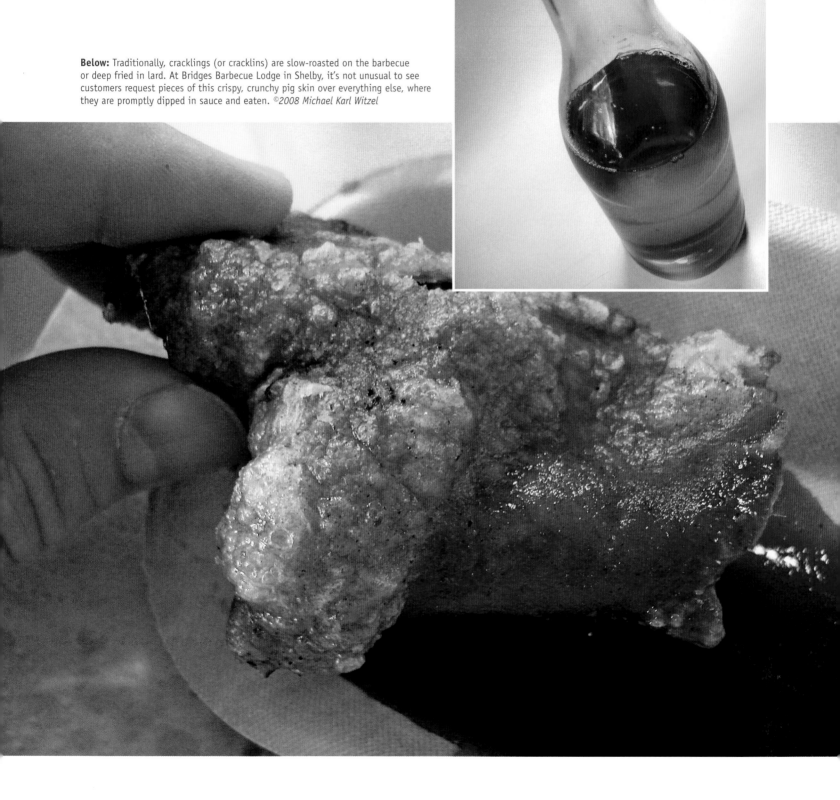

At Bridges Barbecue Lodge, Namon Carlton carefully removes the skin from a pork shoulder fresh from the pits. Once he separates and chops up the meat, he'll add pieces of this "brown" back into the mix to give it more flavor. ©2008 Michael Karl Witzel

Hush puppies are elongated cornbread-dough-batter "nuggets" about the size of small cheese sticks. Deep-fried quickly in a super-hot grease bath, they feature a flavorful golden-brown crust with a yellow and equally flavorful soft middle. Native to North Carolina, hush puppies are rare in other parts of America, although they can be found in some seafood restaurants or other eateries that pay homage to the South. ©2008 Michael Karl Witzel

the label, with a simple list of ingredients printed for all to see. There are no tomatoes here, only vinegar, water, black pepper, red peppers, and spices. In the eastern region of the state, sauce is only used as a moistening agent and to awaken one's taste buds to the flavor of the meat.

"Here, we use a vinegar-based sauce, but as you travel further westward you will see that they serve a tomato-based sauce," Wilber notes. "And that's what the difference between

the east and west is—mainly the sauce. Around here, we've got an old theory that you just don't put vinegar on beef . . . and you don't put ketchup on pork!"

Another regional variation is the addition of what is called outside "brown" to the mix. Brown is the pork skin that is cooked during the process and can be completely savory when it's at its finest. Many barbecue lovers in North Carolina can't have a meal without it and there are even a few places that will

Parker's Barbecue Restaurant Mustard-style Slaw

4–6 pounds of green cabbage, finely chopped
1/2 cup French's yellow mustard
1/4 cup mayonnaise
1/2 cup apple cider vinegar
1/4 cup of sugar
3 tablespoons of celery seed

Chop cabbage on a cutting board and place in a large mixing bowl. In a separate mixing bowl combine the yellow mustard, mayonnaise, apple cider vinegar, sugar and celery seed and mix together until fully blended. Pour this mixture over the cabbage and mix well.

SOURCE: ADAPTED FROM A RECIPE USED AT PARKER'S BARBECUE RESTAURANT, WILSON, NORTH CAROLINA

Wilber's Barbecue has a "family table" occupied by local regulars throughout the day. "They start coming in the morning and that is where all the lies is told and where all the problems are solved," explains Wilber Shirley. "One comes in and one leaves and two come in. It revolves. The only time it is slack is during the lunch crowd. It's the local people, retirees, and some that aren't retirees. They solve all the problems in the world." ©2008 Michael Karl Witzel

Wherever eastern-style North Carolina barbecue is served, it goes without saying that sweetened iced tea—a concoction so strong that a cup or pitcher full of melting ice won't dilute it—will be served with the meal. At Parker's Barbecue in Wilson, Alan Cooper will serve you the whole pitcher straight away, along with plenty of crushed ice and lemon. ©2008 Michael Karl Witzel

sell it to you in pieces. You just dip it in some sauce and eat! Zealots who are unconcerned with cholesterol counts have been known to ask for a "skin sandwich."

But Wilber's is a bit more conservative when it comes to brown. Shirley says, "We don't mix in the brown unless it's just right. And that's what makes our barbecue so different: we mix the ham, the sides, and the shoulder all together when we chop it. Each part of the pig has its own texture. The ham is dryer, the shoulder darker and more greasy, and the sides a whole lot of meat. When you mix it all together, the result is that wonderful, special blend that we serve here."

Inside, the homey, pine-paneled dining room has been known to pack in more than 7,000 customers over a Friday, Saturday, and Sunday stretch. A few years ago, Shirley got a wild hair to put a counter at the front door to record the traffic. "It could be more," he says, since he is unsure if the counter was manning the post the entire time.

Cobbler is one of those traditional Southern desserts that you could just as easily make at home but never do. At Carolina Bar-B-Q in Statesville, the Medlins serve up generous portions of the cherry and blackberry variety to diners with a hankering for a sweet dessert. ©2008 Michael Karl Witzel

The interior decor evokes a real southern feel, with plastic gingham tablecloths completing the down-home look. A few minutes pass and suddenly the table is crowded with a sample of Wilber's foods—a plastic plate with segmented compartments filled with chopped pork, a scoop of potato salad, and some mustard coleslaw. I ask for a Coke, and to my great delight Shirley presents me with the "real thing" in the trademark "Mae West" bottle.

More accustomed to the coarser cuts of meat that are pulled or sliced from pig in the other barbecue regions, I'm surprised to discover that the chopped pork is quite flavorful,

making my mouth water at the pleasantly woodsy, smoky flavor and finishing pleasantly. I pop open a fresh bottle of Wilber's Barbecue Sauce and tentatively splash some onto the meat. After an exploratory nibble, my mouth gradually begins to understand that the combination is excellent. For the first time, I taste the meat and not the sauce.

"There's a friend of mine that I went to school with," Wilber explains. "He's got a place called the Nahunta Pork Center, the nicest in the eastern half of the United States. I buy all of my pork products from him, the whole pig, the bacon, and the sausage." Small world, I think to myself and

Morehead City Famous Tar Heel Hush Puppies

1 pound fine corn meal
1 beaten egg
1 tablespoon salt
1 tablespoon baking soda
1 cup buttermilk

First, pour Wesson oil into a deep fryer and heat to 375 degrees. While deep fryer is preheating, combine all dry ingredients, combine all wet ingredients. Pour the wet ingredients into the flour mixture and stir until blended; mixture will be thick. The mixture needs to be thick but if it is too thick you can add water until it reaches the right consistency (a soft play-dough consistency). Drop in deep fryer by large tablespoons.

Hush puppies will brown up and roll over when they are done. Drain on paper toweling and serve at once (Parker's uses a small amount of sugar in their recipe to help hush puppies brown up and get a little crisper).

SOURCE: THE SANITARY FISH MARKET AND RESTAURANT, MOREHEAD CITY, NORTH CAROLINA, RECIPE DATES FROM THE 1950s

Sonny Conrad, owner and president of the Bar-B-Q Center, serves Lexington-style barbecue in Lexington, North Carolina, cooked in real, wood-fired pits. Here, he shows how the pits are accessed from the outside of the building, through the heavy iron doors of the firebox. ©2008 Michael Karl Witzel

At the Bar-B-Q Center in Lexington, the signature banana splits are legendary both in terms of size and taste. Each boat contains enough ice cream to fill at least four people. ©2008 Michael Karl Witzel

don't mention that fact that I have already been there to gaze at the wonders.

I'm too busy eating, shifting my attention to the little basket of hush puppies that come with every barbecue platter at Wilber's. Since colonial times, the deep-fat-fried cornmeal finger food has been a staple of southern life. Seeing that I enjoy them, Wilber says, "Hush puppies is what makes barbecue."

Wilber is called to the back to assist in the kitchen, but hands me a self-published booklet of Wilber's information before he leaves. Inside is a scrapbook biography of Mr. Shirley and his barbecue restaurant, recounting visits from celebrities like Presidents Bill Clinton and George Bush Sr., along with a long list of others. I grab a bag of hush puppies for the road, along with a bottle of Wilber's Barbecue Sauce, and I'm out the door.

After *National Geographic* proclaimed the Skylight Inn had the best barbecue in the country, Pete Jones decided to let everyone else know that his place was the capital of barbecue. During a remodel of the restaurant, he constructed a replica of the U.S. Capitol dome on top of his roof.
©2008 Michael Karl Witzel

A typical serving at the Skylight Inn consists of a small tray filled with chopped pork, a piece of flat cornbread on top, and a smaller tray of coleslaw cradled on top of that. There are no plates and no unnecessary ceremony when it comes to serving. Here, a serving without brown (the outside skin) is shown at the right, and one with brown to the left. ©2008 Michael Karl Witzel

THE SKYLIGHT INN, AYDEN My next stop is a small tobacco-farming town called Ayden farther east on the map and toward the North Carolina coast. I have directions written on a napkin that I got from Mr. Shirley, but within a few minutes I'm completely lost. The roads are poorly marked, so I'm forced to stop and ask for directions. I finally find my way to N.C. Highway 11 and reach my destination: the Skylight Inn.

There's no sign to speak of on the red brick building, but it's the roof that gets your attention. On top, a scaled down re-creation of the U.S. Capitol rotunda pops against the backdrop of the blue sky. Crowning the silvery, three-tiered layer cake, the stars and stripes flap proudly in the breeze. Over to the far left of the lot there's a small hand-painted billboard that proclaims Pete Jones as the "Bar-B-Q King."

Interestingly enough, the politically inspired architecture has a real connection with barbecue and local elections. Time was in the Tarheel State when politicians held a pig pickin' for their local constituents in order to influence their vote. Political rallies and pig roasts have always been a tradition around here. Today there's no election, but from the number of cars crowding the gravel parking lot, it appears that a large constituency of pork fans have elected to have lunch here.

Once inside, customers walk up to a counter, make a selection, and are handed their food. The menu is limited to barbecue, cornbread, coleslaw, sweet iced tea, and, of course, the usual roster of popular soft drinks. That's it. Here, the barbecue sandwich is boss hog, but you can also order paper barbecue "trays" filled with chopped pork in small, medium, or large sizes.

Behind the counter, a large pass-through window connects directly to the kitchen. At the base of the opening, thick butcher-block surfaces stair-step from the kitchen into the serving area. The blocks aren't flat, but concave, cradling the meat so it doesn't spill onto the floor. Above, a heat lamp radiates a warm glow onto the massive piles of chopped pork, the sight of which triggers the brain centers linked with desire.

After the pork is chopped at the Skylight Inn it moves to the other side of the pass-through window where cook Sergio Darcia makes sandwiches with it or fills small rectangular serving trays with the chop. There's never any reheating here: as fast as the fresh meat is chopped up, it's eaten. ©2008 Michael Karl Witzel

One feature of the Skylight Inn is the large pass-through window between the kitchen and front preparation area. Here, a large butcher-block surface cascades between the two spaces, allowing for minimum effort when it comes to handling the meat. On one side it's chopped, on the other side it's served. *©2008 Michael Karl Witzel*

Within minutes, the large mound of chopped meat is reduced to almost nothing. As fast as the line of hungry customers shuffles through the door and places their orders, the serving staff packs the meat onto trays or piles it onto buns. Some people come from hundreds of miles away to order the chopped delight by the pound, carrying off their 'cue in what the Skylight calls a "two-pound cup" or a "six-pound bucket."

I order a medium-size portion and watch as the countermen work. Moments later, I'm presented with a rectangular paper tray (imprinted with a gingham pattern) filled with chopped pork. On top, they cradle a thick slab of cornbread made with the drippings of barbecued pork. And on top of that, there's another tray of minced coleslaw with a plastic fork stuck into it. There are no trays and you have to carry the stack of containers in one hand and your drink in the other.

At the brown Formica tables, salt and pepper is provided, along with napkins and the obligatory bottle of Texas Pete Hot Sauce, a not too hot, not too mild red pepper–and–vinegar concoction made in nearby Winston-Salem. A second, more mysterious-looking bottle without a label is the house

Emmy Lou Jones, Pete's wife, was the first to make the Skylight Inn's cornbread, inspired by Skilten Dennis' 1830 recipe. Made from a batter of cornmeal, water, salt, and some drippings from barbecued pigs, the hard-crusted bread is flat but soft inside (with the texture of sourdough bread). Skylight Inn cook Wanda Smith pulls trays of cornbread out of the oven after about an hour of baking. ©2008 Michael Karl Witzel

A scene from Bridges Barbecue Lodge in Shelby, North Carolina. The waitresses use the ordering slip to take orders—the closest thing at Bridges to any sort of formal menu. ©2008 Michael Karl Witzel

barbecue "sauce," a rainwater-thin mix made with nothing more than vinegar and water, spices, and the green and red peppers crammed inside the glass container. There's nothing here to hide the flavor of the meat. If the pig ain't cooked right, you'll know it after the first bite.

As I pick up the bottle, turn it slowly in my hands and study the contents, Samuel Jones, the grandson of founder Walter Pete Jones makes his appearance. His father, Bruce Jones, is currently at the Skylight's helm, with other family members on the team. I ask about the sauce and he tells me that he doesn't care for the stuff. "When we cook the pigs, we don't put anything on them at all," he states. "All we have here is the sauce that's on the table. Sauce doesn't make good barbecue . . . and I base that on my granddad's idea that 'It's all in the cooking.' You can put enough sauce on a napkin and eat it. Sauce covers up a mistake."

While I take a sip of my drink and shovel the first forkful of 'cue into my mouth, Samuel gives me the quick history of the Skylight, explaining how the land around the place has been in the Jones family for generations and that they

Chicken, ribs, and chopped pork-—the holy trio of North Carolina barbecue—awaits consumption at Carolina Bar-B-Q in Statesville. ©2008 Michael Karl Witzel

have been making barbecue here for almost a century. As the legend has been handed down across the generations, Sam's great-great-great-grandfather started the whole thing in 1830 when he began selling barbecue out of a covered wagon.

But the business didn't grow roots in this so-called "Collard Capital" of America until 1947, when Sam's grandfather opened the Skylight Inn. Pete was a natural-born barbecue man who some say "had a calling for the business." He daydreamed about owning and running his own barbecue place when he was only in the fifth grade. When he graduated from high school, he stayed in town to work his way into the barbecue trade while others moved away to find fame and fortune.

Samuel says, "It's what he wanted to do. He was a very hard-working man with a work ethic that was beyond most.

He worked every day till he was 76 years old, six days a week. He could outwork me and two others! He would run you in the ground. He had a lot of self-confidence. That was just his character. We'd like to think that we have some of that character in us."

Pete had two uncles who ran restaurants in Ayden and sold barbecue and he worked for one of them for a spell. But that really wasn't enough to satisfy his ambitions, so when he turned 17 he started to build his own place. He was steadfast in his plan and resolute about his success, going so far as to tell one of his uncles that he was going to have "the best barbecue." You can imagine the laughter. Yet another 'cue joint in town.

Turns out that Pete Jones' barbecue bragging wasn't unfounded. In 2003, the Skylight received a James Beard

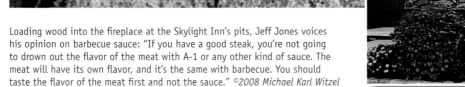

Above: The most distinguishing feature of the Lexington barbecue sandwich is the red coleslaw piled on top of the meat. A balanced combination of cabbage, vinegar, ketchup, and crushed or ground black pepper, red coleslaw is strikingly different than the usual slaw, as it contains no mayonnaise. Lexingtonians (and customers of the Bar-B-Q Center) consider it an essential ingredient to a quality barbecue experience. ©2008 Michael Karl Witzel

Below: At the intersection of U.S. 19 and U.S. 441 in Cherokee, North Carolina, Uncle Ben's Real Pit Barbeque serves up western-style barbecue to North Carolinians in the Great Smoky Mountains. In this region, pork shoulder is favored over whole hog, as is barbecue sauce with ketchup added. *Author's collection*

Loading wood into the fireplace at the Skylight Inn's pits, Jeff Jones voices his opinion on barbecue sauce: "If you have a good steak, you're not going to drown out the flavor of the meat with A-1 or any other kind of sauce. The meat will have its own flavor, and it's the same with barbecue. You should taste the flavor of the meat first and not the sauce." ©2008 Michael Karl Witzel

At the Skylight Inn, James Howell is the master of the flying meat cleavers, wielding two at a time and reducing cooked whole hog into chopped meat within a matter of minutes. ©2008 Michael Karl Witzel

Foundation Culinary Award (in the "Coca-Cola America's Classics" category) and was recently named "Best Barbeque in the South" by *Southern Living* magazine. In 1979, *National Geographic* cited the Skylight Inn as serving the "best barbecue in the world" in a book called *Back Roads of America*. Supposedly, Pete would get a letter from them every year reiterating the fact that no place better had yet been found.

But recognition from the press wasn't the driving force behind Jones' love of the barbecue business. The one thing that satisfied the artisan in him was making barbecue that people craved. That meant sticking to tradition and techniques that worked. "We cook the whole hog here," says Samuel. "That's the way it's done in eastern North Carolina and we think it's the right way, the only way." The hog is split down the middle

and placed on steel bars over the open pit, where it cooks for 13 to 15 hours.

I can tell from the moist, mild-flavored meat that a lot of care and time has gone into making it. The aged wood makes a difference—the Joneses let their hickory weather for six months before they burn it down to coals. The meat is sweet and tender, with sublime, smoky overtones. As an added bonus—and something a newcomer may not appreciate— are the chopped-in flecks of "brown," or pork skin. Along with the white and the dark meat, it forms a complementary blend that really sings. Some may mistake the crunch for bone or gristle, but aficionados know better.

For the culinary-challenged who have grown accustomed to never seeing their food prepared, the process of chopping up the pork quarters is a spectacle to behold. You won't witness anything like it any other eatery in America. Not

Opposite: Whole hog suspended over hot coals is the way they like to do it in the eastern region of North Carolina. It's a long and tedious process, much more difficult to master than the cooking of pork shoulder. If it's not done correctly, the meat will be greasy and inedible. For this reason, it's a craft reserved for pitmasters who know what they are doing. ©2008 Michael Karl Witzel

Bridges Barbecue Lodge was founded in 1946 by Red Bridges, who apprenticed with Lexington barbecue legend Walter Stamey when he lived in the Shelby area. Bridges is one of the great pits of western North Carolina. Until recently, it was operated by Bridges' widow, "Mama B." Today, their only daughter, Debbie Bridges-Webb, is in charge. ©2008 Michael Karl Witzel

only do you get a great sandwich at the Skylight Inn, but a free show as well. Samuel nonchalantly informs me that "We bring the meat out from the pits one quarter of a hog at a time. It'll take about 10 minutes per quarter to chop it up to the consistency that we like, before we serve it."

As we talk, I'm mesmerized by the rhythmic hacking of Mr. James Howell, the hard-workin' man on the other side of the butcher-block pass-through. Like a machine, he alternates two razor sharp meat cleavers in a synchronized ballet of butchery, reducing hunks of pork into fine chop. Every now and then he breaks his rhythm to remove some bone or other "parts," but seconds later gets right back into the endless chopping. In the eastern part of the state, the barbecue is *always* served chopped.

Like the ticking of a clock, the sound takes me back to another time—and another place. For a brief moment, I'm reminded of an American epoch when goods were still made by hand and a hard day's work was rewarded. A time when we

still made things here and didn't just buy them at the local Wal-Mart. The good folks who lived in places like Ayden farmed, raised, or crafted the goods that people bought. Thank God in heaven that they are still making barbecue.

"Back in those days everybody had pigs and farmed tobacco," says Samuel. "At the end of the season, after all of the tobacco and cotton were in, they'd have—and pardon me if this sounds a little bit redneck—what some called a 'hog killing.' All the people who had worked on the farm that year were invited. Every part of the pig was used up, too. They'd get the lard out, and some would cook the innards. They'd make hams and hang them up to cure in the smokehouse. For the barbecue, it was as simple as digging a hole in the ground,

At Bridges Barbecue Lodge in Shelby, North Carolina, Namon Carlton watches over the production of the pork shoulder, the primary ingredient of this eatery's staple dishes: chopped or sliced barbecue and barbecue pork sandwiches. ©2008 Michael Karl Witzel

filling it with burning hickory coals, putting a piece of wire over it, and laying the pig on it."

With that history lesson, the afternoon sun is getting low in the sky and I'm compelled to keep my schedule. I thank Samuel for the barbecue—and a true taste of what the eastern half of the state has to offer—and tell him that the pork was an equal match for any Texas brisket, Memphis ribs, or Kansas City burnt ends. What I don't tell him is that I'm heading 'cross the state's barbecue dividing line into enemy pitmaster territory.

LEXINGTON BARBECUE, LEXINGTON

"North Carolina's well-held myth says that the state's dueling barbecue styles are separated by the 'Gnat Line', an invisible barrier that separates the sandy soil that attracted gnats to the east and the denser rocky and clay soil of the Piedmont Region to the west," wrote Manuel Roig-Franzia in a 2005 article in the *Washington Post*. The dividing line is more than myth, but a true cultural divide that pits one region against the other. The city of Raleigh straddles the line.

A few years back, a North Carolina state representative even proposed that the popular barbecue festival that was held every year in Lexington be recognized as the state's "official" barbecue festival. The idea went over as big as a pork shoulder cooked over Kingsford briquettes on a hibachi. The festival ended up being called the state's official "food fest" and the fires of discontent died down.

Lexington Style "Red" Slaw

There are many variations on the "red" slaw recipe; some include barbecue sauce instead of catsup, others add brown sugar, and still others include green peppers and onions. This recipe is an adaptation of the slaw that is served at the Lexington Barbecue.

According to Wayne Monk, president of Lexington Barbecue Incorporated, this is "just a ballpark" estimation of the measurements. You might want to go easy on the cayenne and increase it to taste. The original recipe calls for about 1-1/2 ounces of ground red pepper to 10 pounds of cabbage, making this slaw on the spicy side.

5 pounds green or white cabbage, chopped fine
2-1/2 teaspoons of salt
1-1/2 teaspoons black ground pepper
1-1/2 tablespoons ground red pepper (cayenne) or to taste
1 cup sugar + 1 tablespoon
2 cups catsup
1 cup vinegar

Chop cabbage on a cutting board and place in a large mixing bowl. In a separate bowl combine the catsup, vinegar, salt, pepper and cayenne together. Pour over cabbage and mix well. Refrigerate and let sit at least 2 hours before serving.

SOURCE: WAYNE MONK, LEXINGTON BARBECUE, LEXINGTON, NORTH CAROLINA

From the rear of Lexington Barbecue's lot, one may witness the grandeur of the six barbecue pit smokestacks used to vent the ovens inside—clear evidence that Wayne Monk's place is no fly-by-night operation. ©2008 Michael Karl Witzel

Nevertheless, the city of Lexington, North Carolina, like so many other cities throughout the South, has been christened "The Barbecue Capital of the World." It claims to have the world's highest per capita concentration of barbecue consumption, with some 17 restaurants serving 20,000 residents. One of the restaurants is owned by Mr. Wayne Monk and takes the same name as the city itself: Lexington Barbecue.

Once again, I find a parking lot that's packed with cars, motorcycles, and motorhomes, with nary a space left over to park my cowboy Cadillac. Young and old—every race, creed, and color—wait patiently in a long line that starts in the parking lot, goes through the front door, and ends at the hostess. Some forgo the wait and take a stool at the small lunch counter, which is my first choice. "We've been coming to Lexington for more than 15 years," announces a devotee sitting on the stool next to me, as he finishes a golden hush puppy. "After the game,

When motorists see the familiar Lexington Barbecue sign, they know they are in the western half of the state's two barbecue regions. For many, the state's self-appointed 'cue line is pretty much drawn at the city of Raleigh. ©2008 Michael Karl Witzel

Lexington-style Pulled Pork

Part One
Pork butt, Boston butt, or untrimmed end-cut pork shoulder roast, 7–9 pounds
Olive oil
Kosher salt
Freshly ground pepper
Hickory wood chips, soaked in water for 30 minutes
Lexington-style Vinegar Sauce (recipe below)
North Carolina Coleslaw
8 plain white hamburger buns

Procedure
1. Build a charcoal or gas grill for indirect cooking.
2. Do not trim any excess fat off the meat; this fat will naturally baste the meat and keep it moist during the long cooking time. Brush pork with a thin coating of olive oil. Season with salt and pepper. Set aside on a clean tray until ready to cook.
3. Before placing the meat on the grill, add the soaked wood chips. Place the chips directly on gray-ashed briquettes or in the smoking box of your gas grill. If you are using a charcoal grill, you will need to add charcoal every hour to maintain the heat.
4. Place the pork in the center of the cooking grate, fat-side up, over indirect low heat. Cover and cook slowly for 4–5 hours at 325 degrees to 350 degrees, or until an instant-read thermometer inserted into the middle of the pork registers 190 degrees to 200 degrees. The meat should be very tender and falling apart. If there is a bone in the meat, it should come out smooth and clean with no meat clinging to it.
5. Let the meat rest for 20 minutes or until cool enough to handle. Using rubber kitchen gloves, pull the meat from the skin, bones, and fat. Set aside the crispy bits (fat) that have been rendered and look almost burned. Working quickly, shred the chunks of meat with two forks and "pulling" the meat into small pieces from the butt. Alternately, you can chop the meat with a cleaver. Chop the reserved crispy bits and mix into the pulled pork. While the meat is still warm, mix with enough Lexington-style Vinegar Sauce to moisten and season the meat (about 3/4 cup).
6. Serve hot, sandwich-style on a hamburger bun and top with coleslaw. Serve more sauce on the side if desired.

Serves: 10

---

the tradition is that we all meet up here to eat barbecue." Tonight, it appears that everyone else has the same idea. The Lexington is slowly bursting at the seams.

I alert the hostess to my presence and a few moments later, Wayne Monk steps through the swinging kitchen door and out into the frenzy. A service-oriented gem of a barbecue man, his easygoing smile and warm demeanor are as comforting as the food he serves. He starts at the beginning, telling me that on his sixteenth birthday he landed his first job at a restaurant run by a man named Holland Tussey. It was the early 1950s.

His job as a curb hop—a parking lot waiter who brought food and drinks to people dining in their cars—was nothing glamorous. Working for tips, it was a constant hustle running back and forth between the kitchen and the cars. During quiet times, he kept busy by picking up trash in the parking lot. It didn't take too much of that for Monk to realize that he wanted to move up the food chain. Soon, he was working inside at the counter and occasionally in the kitchen.

"Mr. Tussey cooked barbecue, so sometimes he would let me carry the meat from the cooler to the pit," Monk recalls. "Or, put the meat on the pit and fire it for the first time. As the years passed, I realized there was a particular sense of pride that came with preparing barbecue in Lexington . . . and that sort of influenced my future direction. Eventually, I took hold of that pride and realized that this is what I wanted to specialize in."

By 1962, Monk had the experience he needed and secured a barbecue place of his own. After Thanksgiving of that year, he fired up his own pit, but soon discovered that pride isn't enough to carry a business. "I actually started out on a wing and a prayer," admits Monk. "At the time, I didn't have enough money to buy this place so I had to take a partner. But we didn't

Part Two
Lexington-style Vinegar Sauce
2 cups apple cider vinegar
1/2 cup ketchup
1/4 cup packed brown sugar
2 tablespoons sugar
1 tablespoon kosher salt
1 tablespoon ground white pepper
1/2–1 tablespoon red pepper flakes
1/2 teaspoon freshly ground black pepper

Mix all ingredients together in a large glass bowl
and let sit at least 10 minutes or almost indefinitely,
covered in the refrigerator.

Makes about 3 cups

Source: www.seriouseats.com

If you live in Charlotte or Greensboro,
you are still local to Lexington Barbecue.
Located on a major Interstate, Lexington
Barbecue gets Charlotte business once
or twice a week, especially if people are
passing through on their way to a ballgame
at UNC, or Duke, or NC State. On the way
back, they might stop and eat again and
take a pound or two home with them.
©2008 Michael Karl Witzel

With its retro dining table and chairs and vinyl-padded booths, the interior of Bridges Barbecue Lodge resembles an upscale 1950s diner more than it does a lodge, but then again, this is no lodge for spending the night, but rather one designed for the sole purpose of dining on barbecue. ©2008 Michael Karl Witzel

Lexington Barbecue offers carhop service to its customers. Proprietor Wayne Monk got his first job as a curb hop and worked his way up from there to build one of Lexington's most famous barbecue businesses. At Lexington, carhop Russ Craver works the cars. ©2008 Michael Karl Witzel

have the business we needed and the money wasn't there, so one of us had to go." Monk bought out the other fellow.

There were other challenges. He had no air-conditioning and only had one barbecue pit that leaked smoke into his dining room. He folds his hands and smiles, telling me "In the beginning, we were trying to be a little better each day. We had no real business goals, just to do a better job tomorrow—to handle a little more volume tomorrow—and, of course, to make a little bit more money tomorrow. It was a simple plan, but that was pretty much our philosophy."

As he mixed pride with endurance and added a dash of patience, one thing remained true: barbecue prepared and served in the Lexington tradition. Pork shoulder is what they call barbecue on this side of the Gnat Line, and no one minds if you slice off the occasional piece. It also means that no one is going to have a nervous breakdown in the dining room if they happen to find a little bit of ketchup mixed into the coleslaw, and that no one is going to give you dirty looks if you happen to like barbecue sauce that has some tomato product added to the recipe.

And of course, using coals made from burning real wood is the only way to cook in Lexington. "We cook on a pit," Monk explains. "We have a firebox where we actually burn the oak and hickory wood and shovel it out and put it directly under the meat. We also prefer the pork shoulders—nothing else but shoulders—in this area. It's a very labor-intensive way of cooking, but that is what we like to do. We think it's the best, we like the cut of meat, and we take quite a bit of pride in that. And it is sooo good!"

Today, Monk doesn't talk about pride all that much. His restaurant does all the talking for him. The single pit of the early days has multiplied into four massive units, each with its own smokestack rising from the rear of the building. For

Opposite: Pitmaster Phillip Schenck works well into the wee hours at Bridges Barbecue Lodge to make sure that the pork will be properly cooked and ready for the next day's business. ©2008 Michael Karl Witzel

Lexington-style barbecue is made with pork shoulder cooked slowly over a hardwood fire, usually hickory. It's basted in a sauce called "dip" made with vinegar, ketchup, water, salt, pepper, and a few other spices. Ingredients vary from restaurant to restaurant, and most recipes are secret. As Lexington Barbecue owner Wayne Monk shows here, customers enjoy it on buns, or simply paired up with a big scoop of red slaw. ©2008 Michael Karl Witzel

Lexington Barbecue employs three Ricks. One of them, Rick Earnhardt, does the majority of the cooking and the meat chopping on the heavy butcher-block table in the rear of the kitchen. On this shift, Caylen Wall mans the chopping block. ©2008 Michael Karl Witzel

each fire pit, there's an inside and an outside door. The wood is loaded from the outside in 2-foot-long slabs and burns down to hot coals that are pushed deeper into the pit. When the red-hot coals lose their heat, the remains are shoveled out from the other side. The heat is so intense inside that even the thick metal pit doors are warped.

The sheer volume of meat cooked in these pits gives Monk the flexibility to prepare his pork according to the whims of customers. "We take the pork shoulder apart," says Monk.

"You can get the more fatty brown outside meat, which has more flavor and smoke, or you get the lean white inside meat, without brown and no smoked flavor at all. You can get it chopped, you can get it sliced, and you can get big hunks. If you want fat, we will serve it to you." It's no surprise that a third of the Lexington's orders are special ones.

Pulled and sliced pork are available in North Carolina, but the majority of establishments prefer to prepare their pork by chopping it into a loose mince, using dual meat cleavers as a human-powered food processor. ©2008 Michael Karl Witzel

But whether it's light meat or dark, Monk explains that the pork shoulder has to be cooked a certain way or none of it will taste right. "We start off with what we call the 'face'," he says, "the side that doesn't have skin on it. We brown it on the other side. On some pits it will take you two hours, others three. You brown the front, turn it over, and then brown it a little bit heavier on the back. That's when you get all these drippings.

"The final phase of the cooking is where we turn it over, fire it lightly, and allow the meat to drip evenly." Monk gets serious and says, "The draining is important. If you don't know what you are doing, the meat will be greasy and have a bad flavor." After that, the meat is moved to another pit where it rests for about two hours. During this time, it cooks a little bit more and gets even more tender. Monk clenches his fist to emphasize a point and explains, "When you first get through with the cooking, the meat is like a tight fist. When it rests, the muscles relax . . . and it's easier to eat."

I'm relaxed as well—and ready to eat. I ask Monk if I can try the Lexington-style barbecue sandwich with a mix of white and dark meat. He scribbles my order on one of those little green diner ordering pads and clips it onto a revolving holder mounted above a pass-through. It spins around and is grabbed by someone in the kitchen. A few minutes later, my cork-lined tray filled with food slides out.

Lexington calls itself "The Barbecue Capital of the World." Since 1984, the city has hosted the Lexington Barbecue Festival, one of the largest street festivals in North Carolina. The city boasts more than 20 barbecue restaurants: an average of more than one per thousand residents. At Wayne Monk's Lexington Barbecue, counter service is the quickest to get your fill. ©2008 Michael Karl Witzel

Opposite above: At Lexington Barbecue, customers can order their meat custom blended. If you like your chopped pork with flavorful outside "brown," they will add it in according to your taste. If you like your pork without brown, they will serve it that way too. Here, everything is made to order, just the way you like it. ©2008 Michael Karl Witzel

Opposite below: According to Wayne Monk, there are about 15 barbecue restaurants within 5 miles of Lexington Barbecue but "only a third of them are really doing a real volume business." At Lexington, servers like Tammy Rhodes are always busy, juggling trays and shuttling orders of food to the customers nonstop. ©2008 Michael Karl Witzel

North Carolina-style Brunswick Stew

Many Brunswick stew recipes are on the sweet side because they add canned creamed corn to the mixture and use ketchup. Others use bacon, and still others use hot sauce, and Worcestershire sauce. However, this recipe is an approximation of one shared with me by Donald Williams of Parker's Barbecue with the exception that they use Old Mansion Brunswick Stew seasoning in theirs. If you can find this seasoning in your area by all means use it.

For their 20-gallon stew, Parker's uses a one-pound container of this seasoning and thickening mix. This recipe makes approximately 10 gallons. If you want to spice it up you can always add Worcestershire sauce or hot sauce to the mixture.

5–7 pounds stewing hens
4 quarts cold water
1 cup celery, diced
5 large yellow onions, chopped
3 medium potatoes, peeled and diced
2 1-pound cans lima beans (drained)
1 1-pound can whole kernel corn (drained)
3 1-pound cans tomato puree
4 1-pound cans string beans (drained)
1 teaspoon salt
3/4 teaspoon pepper
1 stick margarine
3/4 cup flour

Cut chicken into pieces and simmer in a 4-quart pot of water for 2–4 hours until meat falls from bone. Remove meat from water, strain and reserve the stock, keeping back about 1 quart or just enough to cover the diced potatoes, celery, and onions. Using the same pot, add back stock to cover raw vegetables and simmer celery, onions, and potatoes until potatoes are tender.

While this is simmering, remove chicken meat from bones by pulling it, hand shredding or dicing it into small pieces (hand shredding is preferred method). Add the tomato puree to pot and bring to a simmer and add the spices. In a small pan melt the margarine, adding flour with a wire whisk; whisk until smooth, being careful not to burn this mixture. Slowly add the flour mixture to the pot, whisking or stirring until the mixture is well blended. Then add the chicken meat and drained canned vegetables to the pot and allow to simmer an additional 15 minutes.

This recipe is best prepared a day in advance before serving. Serve up with corn sticks or hush puppies.

SOURCE: ADAPTED FROM A RECIPE USED AT PARKER'S BARBECUE RESTAURANT, WILSON, NORTH CAROLINA

The sandwich is made with a large burger bun, piled with mixed morsels of chopped pork, just as I ordered. A generous layer of crimson-tinged cabbage is layered on top. Unaccustomed to the Lexington-style sandwich, I take my first tentative bite and am pleasantly surprised. The combination is a winner, the zesty slaw blending nicely with the smoky pork. I abandon my table manners and chomp through the delectable dish, alternating between hush puppies and sandwich, washing it all down with oh-so-sweet tea.

At the Lexington, the food has been like this for decades, and Monk isn't about to change anything soon. He says, "I have a lot of involvement and the desire to keep things the way they are. I am stubborn enough, and I'm not changing."

He still serves the same barbecue, but also sells a fair amount of ground chuck, hot dogs, hush puppies, and French fries. Some of his customers come in to eat four or five times a week, so he has to maintain variety. In his humble opinion, he feels that if you give the public what they want—and the service to go along with it—they will keep on coming back again and again and again.

"One of the things that I really love about this business is the people, my customers," says Monk. "These days, I am literally

This stronghold of Lexington-style barbecue began many years ago across the street from its current location as a dairy center that served ice cream. Today, with its quaint 1950s soda-fountain interior and relaxed atmosphere, the Bar-B-Q Center is the place that most of the locals head to when they crave barbecue and an old-fashioned milkshake. ©2008 Michael Karl Witzel

At Bridges Barbecue Lodge, there's nothing like having a Sundrop soda with your barbecue pork. Charles Lazier, a salesman of beverage concentrates, developed the brand in St. Louis in 1949. Over the years, Sundrop developed a loyal customer base because of its unique citrus flavor. In many Southeastern states, Sundrop was known as Sun-drop Golden Cola, Golden Girl Cola, and Golden Sun-drop Cola. ©2008 Michael Karl Witzel

waiting on the third generation. Believe it or not, some of the people that I am waiting on today are the same people that I first waited on when I was first working as a curb hop! And I take pride in that—that they'll follow me . . . you know? *And* eat with me over the years. I get high just thinking about that."

By this time, I'm high, too—high on sweet tea and barbecue and the simple fact that this amazing genre of food—the way it has evolved into the cultish category of food that it is now, along with its many tricks and techniques, myths and secrets,

promises and dreams—is so American in nature. Monk's story has taken me to the zenith of the barbecue world and Lexington Barbecue has turned out to be more than I ever expected.

I know that one day I will be back, just like his loyal crowd of locals, so I say "*auf wiedersehen*" instead of goodbye. I'm really going to miss the kind of 'cue they make in the Tarheel State and the evident passion that goes into making it.

Esse quam videri is North Carolina's state motto, and it could not be more appropriate, for it translates into "To be, rather than to seem," a slogan that applies to barbecue in spades. North Carolina is a barbecue region of the highest order. Among the four regions of legendary American barbecue, it doesn't just play around with the idea of pork barbecue, but defines the art, and lives it.

Banana Pudding

After chowing down on a rack of ribs, a plate of brisket, a pulled-pork sandwich, or a platter of fat sausage links, one's thoughts inevitably turn grudgingly away from barbecue and toward something sweet.

The question is: what dessert can provide the perfect counterbalance to the inherent smokiness of the barbecue meal and tickle the palate in just the right way? For many aficionados, the question is moot. Nothing less than a big ol' heaping bowl of banana pudding will do the trick.

But the banana's journey from the tropical groves of South America to the dessert carts of the Deep South was a long one. As the Chiquita Company tells the tale, Captain Lorenzo Dow Baker was the first to import bananas in 1870, when he bought 160 bunches in Jamaica. Eleven days later he sold them in Jersey City, New Jersey, to great commotion.

Even so, fruit historians report that bananas were officially introduced to Americans at the Philadelphia Centennial Exhibition in 1876. There, each banana was wrapped in foil and sold for 10 cents, a considerable chunk of change for the time. But a steady supply and an indifferent demand drove down prices. By 1910, the once-foreign banana was so common that it joined the pantheon of other domestic fruits in ubiquity.

It's easy to see why, since bananas were recommended by promoters as the secret to longevity, the perfect food for infants, and the cure for warts. At the same time, it was reported that they cured headaches and stage fright.

Grandiose claims aside, creative cooks of the era developed much more practical—and flavorful—uses for the fruit that came packaged in its own wrapper. Slowly, everyone from professional chefs to amateur cooks began incorporating bananas into their recipes, in search of the next big taste sensation.

In 1902, *Mrs. Rorer's New Cook Book* by Sarah Tyson Rorer featured "Hawaiian Recipes" for fried and baked bananas, banana pudding, and even banana cake. Other recipe books followed suit with their own concoctions. It didn't take long for someone to discover that vanilla custard was the perfect mate for sliced bananas. After the Nabisco Company began marketing vanilla wafers in 1901, all of the elements were in place.

Through some serendipitous course of events, the custard and sliced bananas found their way into a bowl layered and lined with vanilla wafers and topped with a frothy layer of meringue or whipped cream. This was it: a dreamy, creamy combination of flavors that pleased even the most discriminating dessert addict.

Touted as "Quite Possibly the World's Perfect Food," the banana—in the form of banana pudding—rose from obscurity to become a standard after-dinner treat throughout the South. In the minds of barbecue lovers, it could be called the world's most perfect dessert.

A textbook example of old-fashioned banana pudding, created at Corky's BBQ, Memphis, Tennessee. ©2008 Michael Karl Witzel

North Carolina 'Cue Shrine
Parker's Barbecue

2514 U.S. Highway 301 South
Wilson, North Carolina 27893
(252) 237-0972

A vintage postcard from 1952 depicts Parker's Barbecue as a simple white building with a full parking lot and a neon sign at the front. Since then, little has changed at this long-standing eastern North Carolina fixture—inside or out. Southern hospitality is everywhere, mirrored in the pleasant faces of employees. Waiters, donned with white-cap hats straight out of the 1950s, scurry about with trays of food and pitchers of sweet tea garnished with lemon wedges. The atmosphere is no-frills, but it feels like home and family.

On a busy Sunday, the after-church crowd mingles with out-of-towners as a steady stream of people fill up the dining hall. Here, time is measured slow and steady, not by the hour or the minute hand, but by the pounds of meat served and the gallons of iced tea poured.

It's a place where comfort food is spelled out plainly for folks: fried chicken, better than Mama's; flavorful chopped barbecue pork; sweet hush puppies; fried corn sticks; thick and hearty Brunswick stew; paprika-boiled potatoes, just like Grandma made; and a new arrival on the menu: string beans.

When I asked Donald Williams, current president of Parker's, why he recently added the string beans to the menu he replies, "Well, everybody kept asking me for string beans, so I decided that we'd go ahead and put string beans on the menu."

"When was that?" I asked. "Oh . . . probably been about 15 years ago."

Turns out that the hush puppies are another "new" item, only recently added—22 years ago. This is not a place that messes with tradition—anything less than 30 years old is considered "new."

Parker's was founded in August 1946 by brothers Graham and Ralph Parker along with their cousin, Henry Parker Brewer. Like most young men in this tobacco-growing area, they were from farming stock, but after a stint in the service they decided to open up a barbecue restaurant. A loan from the bank funded their startup and they saved money by using wood cut from their father's farm to build the restaurant. Their choice of location along U.S. Highway 301 turned out to be fortuitous: the postwar years boomed, bringing locals, tourists, truckers, and other travelers discovering the open road right to their front door.

Another wave of good fortune occurred in 1954 when Ralston Purina opened up nearby. The company hired Parker's to feed over 17,000 people at their grand opening. Ralston paid 75 cents a plate and handed Parker's Barbecue a check for $12,750. That was a lot of money back then—more money than any of them had ever seen. Immediately, they paid off the bank. From that point on, Parker's was on rock-solid financial ground.

Then, in 1963, a fresh-faced boy just out of high school entered the working ranks at Parker's, waiting tables. At the time Donald Williams had little notion of what the future would bring, he just knew he enjoyed his job. Soon he was doing more than waiting tables. He graduated to cook and by the 1970s was managing the place. When Henry Parker Brewer died in 1987, the Parker brothers decided to retire, and Williams was ready. He and Bobby Woodward (another long-time employee at Parker's) stepped in as the new owners. That was 20 years ago.

(continued overleaf)

Circa 1952 postcard. Prior to the American Civil War, it was estimated that the typical Southerner ate 5 pounds of pork for every pound of beef. Not only that, hard times resulted in every part of the pig being eaten or saved for later, including the ears, feet, and organs. Since 1942, Parker's in Wilson, North Carolina, has done its best to ensure the vitality of those early estimates. *Author's collection*

After Bobby Woodward died, Williams took two new business partners: Eric Lippard, a Parker's employee of 19 years, and Kevin Lamm, a Parker's employee of 22 years. Together, they run one of the most successful restaurants in this part of the country. It shows in every facet of their business, and if you take a look at what goes on behind the scenes, it's like watching a harmonious family at work.

Each segment of the operation is manned by a small group of people, expert in their area. It's been that way ever since Williams started working here in 1963. In fact, one of the cooks, who is now semiretired, has been working here for 58 years! Several others have been working at Parker's for 30 years.

At the back of this operation is a focus on detail and quality ingredients. Everything is made fresh daily, on the premises, including Parker's tangy-sweet coleslaw. Buckets of potatoes ready for boiling sit in containers of water. There's a store room designated just for cabbage, and meat lockers hold the pork in a state of suspended animation.

A separate building houses the pits where the pork is barbecued. This operation takes place after hours when the restaurant is closed to the public. At this time, a new crew steps in and takes over, placing the halved-pigs onto the gas-fired pits at 9 p.m. By 6 a.m. the pigs are ready to be deboned and chopped. The skins are actually deep fried—similar to pork rinds—and chopped up and mixed back into the barbecue, giving Parker's barbecue its unique texture and depth of flavor.

Parker's adds a vinegar sauce mixture consisting of 2 quarts of apple cider vinegar, 1/2 cup salt, and 1/3 cup crushed red peppers to each 30 pounds of chopped meat. It's been done this way for decades at Parker's, except for a brief period when they used a wood-and-charcoal mixture in its pits. The pits were converted to gas during the 1950s and have remained basically the same ever since.

At Parker's, there are no surprises, and that's the main attraction. You know just what you are getting—the taste, the texture, and the service—every time you come to eat. You're also surrounded by familiar faces, and not just those of your neighbors—the people who work here have become, over the years, a second family. "I've been in the business since I was 17," says Williams, "and what always makes me happy when I get through with the day is that my customers are satisfied."

Parker's is all about good food and Southern hospitality . . . and it doesn't get any better than that.

Above left: At Parker's, who says you can't have your barbecue and eat it, too? It's all here: fried chicken, chopped pork, Brunswick stew, boiled potatoes, corn sticks, and coleslaw. ©2008 Michael Karl Witzel

Above right: Inside, Parker's Barbecue looks a lot like it did 20 years ago. Dining-room servers (all young men) like Michael Aycock are dressed in white uniforms complete with paper hats reminiscent of a more vintage dining establishment. ©2008 Michael Karl Witzel

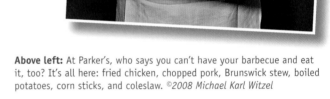

Four miles off of I-95 on U.S. 301 north of U.S. 264 (the road to the Outer Banks), Parker's Barbecue has evolved since 1946 into an institution in the small North Carolina town of Wilson. For about five bucks, you get a large dinner plate of barbecue complete with side orders of Brunswick stew or green beans, boiled potatoes or French fries, or coleslaw and corn sticks. ©2008 Michael Karl Witzel

Top: At Parker's Barbecue in Wilson, Donald Williams and Eric Lippard stock a ready supply of pork in its own cooler. ©2008 Michael Karl Witzel

Left: At Parker's Barbecue in Wilson, the fried chicken has gained a loyal following of its own. Baskets full of the breaded poultry are fried in a long line of fryers manned by exuberant and motivated cooks like Bobby Battle. ©2008 Michael Karl Witzel

Above: At Parker's, the original pits used a wood-and-charcoal mixture. However, the pits were converted to gas during the 1950s and have remained the same since (shown here with Donald Wilson). During the cooking process, the metal canopy is lowered to waist level by an electric motor. ©2008 Michael Karl Witzel

BARBECUE RESTAURANT GUIDE

This guide is not intended as a restaurant rating, nor is this a complete index of all the barbecue restaurants in a particular region or state. Its only purpose is to provide information to the reader on the name and location of barbecue restaurants located throughout the United States.

The restaurants listed in this guide were chosen on the basis of length of time in business and/or popularity. We regret that space does not allow us to list each state and every town and city within a particular state. We also apologize in advance if your favorite 'cue joint was not included.

NORTH CAROLINA
"Eastern style"

Allen & Son Barbecue
6203 Millhouse Road
Chapel Hill, NC 27516
(919) 942-7576

A&M Grill
401 E. Center Street
Mebane, NC 27302
(919) 563-3721

B's Barbecue, Greenville
751 B's Barbecue Road
Greenville, NC 27834

Bill Ellis Barbecue
3007 Downing Street Extension
Wilson, NC 27896
(252) 237-4372

Fuzzy's
111 West Murphy Street
Madison, NC 27025
(336) 427-4130

Grady's Barbecue
3096 Arrington Bridge Road
Dudley, NC 28333
(919) 735-7243

Hursey's Barbecue
1834 South Church Street
Burlington, NC 27215
(336) 226-1694

Moore's Barbecue
3711 U.S. Highway 17S
New Bern, NC 28562
(252) 638-3937

Parker's Barbecue
2514 U.S. Highway 3015
Wilson, NC 27893
(252) 237-0972

Stamey's Barbecue
2206 High Point Road
Greensboro, NC 27403
(336) 299-9888

Stephenson's Barbecue
11964 N.C. Highway 50 North
Willow Springs, NC 27592
(919) 894-4530

Short Sugar's Drive-In
1328 South Scales Street
Reidsville, NC 27320
(336) 342-7487

The Skylight Inn
4618 Lee Street
Ayden, NC 28513
(252) 746-4113

Wilber's Barbecue
4172 U.S. Highway 70 East
Goldsboro, NC 27534
(919) 778-5218

NORTH CAROLINA
"Western style"

Bridge's Barbecue Lodge
2000 E. Dixon Boulevard
Shelby, NC 28152
(704) 482-8567

Carolina Bar-B-Q
213 Salisbury Road
Statesville, NC 28677
(704) 873-5585

Deano's Barbecue
140 N. Clement Street
Mocksville, NC 27028
(336) 751-5820

Herb's Pit BBQ,
15735 West U.S. 64
Murphy, NC 28906
(828) 494-5367

Hill's Lexington Barbecue
4005 North Patterson Avenue
Winston-Salem, NC 27105
(336) 767-2184

Lexington Barbecue
10 Highway 29-70 South
Lexington, NC 27295
(336) 249-9814

Little Pigs of America
384 Mcdowell Street
Asheville, NC 28803
(828) 254-4253

Little Richard's Bar-B-Que
4885 Country Club Road
Winston-Salem, NC 27104
(336) 760-3457

M&K Barbecue & Country Cooking
215 North Salisbury Avenue
Granite Quarry, NC 28072
(704) 279-8976

Richard's Bar-B-Q
522 North Main Street
Salisbury, NC 28144
(704) 636-9561

Short Sugar's Pit Bar-B-Q
1328 South Scales Street
Reidsville, NC 27320
(910) 342-7487

Speedy Lohr's BBQ of Arcadia
8000 North Highway 150
Enterprise Road
Lexington, NC 27295
(336) 764-5509

The Barb-B-Q Center, Inc.
900 North Main Street
Lexington, NC 27292
(336) 248-4633

Wink's Bar-B-Que
509 Faith Road
Salisbury, NC 28146-7011
(704) 637-2410

TENNESSEE BARBECUE
"Memphis-style"

A&R Bar-B-Que
1802 Elvis Presley Boulevard
Memphis, TN 38106
(901) 774-7444

Brown's Bar-B-Q
1061 South Third Street
Memphis, TN 38106
(901) 942-2941

Bryant's Bar-b-q
3965 Summer Avenue
Memphis, TN 38122
(901) 324-7494

Corky's Bar-B-Q
5259 Poplar Avenue
Memphis, TN 38119
(901) 685-9744

Cozy Corner Restaurant
745 North Parkway
Memphis, TN 38105
(901) 527-9158

Jim Neeley's Interstate Bar-B-Que
2265 South Third Street
Memphis, TN 38109
(901) 775-2304

Leonard's Pit Barbecue
5465 Fox Plaza Drive
Memphis, TN 38115
(901) 360-1963

71

Little Pigs Bar-B-Q
671 South Highland Street
Memphis, TN 38111
(901) 323-9433

Marlowe's Ribs & Restaurant
4381 Elvis Presley Boulevard
Memphis, TN 38116
(901) 332-4159

Neely's Bar-B-Que Restaurant
670 Jefferson Avenue
Memphis, TN 38105
(901) 521-9798

Payne's Bar-B-Q
1762 Lamar Avenue
Memphis, TN 38114
(901) 272-1523

Payne's Bar-B-Q
1393 Elvis Presley Boulevard
Memphis, TN 38106
(901) 942-7433

Rendezvous
52 South Second Street
Memphis, TN 38103
(901) 523-2746

TThe Bar-B-Q Shop
1782 Madison Avenue
Memphis, TN 38104
(901) 272-1277

Three Little Pigs Bar-B-Q
5145 Quince Road
Memphis, TN 38117
(901) 685-7094

Tom's Bar-B-Que
4087 Getwell Road
Memphis, TN 38118
(901) 365-6690

Tops Bar-B-Q
2748 Lamar
Memphis TN 38107
(901) 743-3480

TEXAS
"Texas style"

Angelo's
2533 White Settlement Road
Fort Worth, TX
(817) 332-0357

Black's BBQ
215 North Main Street
Lockhart, TX 78644
(512) 398-2712

City Market
633 East Davis Street
Luling, TX 78648
(830) 875-9019

Cooper's Old Time Pit Bar B Que
506 West Young Street
Llano, TX 78643
(915) 247-5713

Goode Company Barbeque
5109 Kirby Drive
Houston, TX 77098
(713) 522-2530

Hammond's B-B-Q
1106 NE Big Bend Trail
Glen Rose, TX 76043
(254) 897-3008

J & J BBQ
1306 TX Avenue
Lubbock, TX 79401
(806) 744-1325

Joe Allen's BBQ
301 South 11th Street
Abilene, TX 79602
(325) 672-6082

Kirby's Barbeque
216 N Highway 14
Mexia, TX 76667
(254) 562-5076

Kreuz Market
619 North Colorado Street
Lockhart, TX 78644
(512) 398-2361

Lone Star Bar B Q
2010 South Bridge Street
Brady, TX 76825
(915) 597-1936

Louie Mueller Barbecue
206 West 2nd Street
Taylor, TX 76574
(512) 352-6206

Miss Mae's Bar-B-Q
419 FM 2325
Wimberley TX 78676
(512) 847-9808

North Main Bar BQ
406 North Main Street
Euless, TX 76039
(817) 283-0884

Peggy Sue BBQ
6600 Snider Plaza
Dallas, TX 75205
(214) 987-9188

Queen's Bar-B-Que
35th and Avenue S
Galveston, TX 77550
(409) 762-3151

Riscky's Barbeque
140 East Exchange Avenue
Fort Worth, TX 76106
(817) 626-7777

Rudy's Country Store and Bar-B-Q
24152 West IH 10
San Antonio, TX 78257
(210) 698-2141

Smitty's Market
208 South Commerce Street
Lockhart, TX 78644
(512) 398-9344

Sonny Bryan's Smokehouse
2202 Inwood Road
Dallas, TX 75235
(214) 357-7120

Soulman's Barbeque
3410 Broadway Boulevard
Garland, TX 75043
(972) 271-6885

Stubbs BBQ
801 Red River Street
Austin, TX 78701
(512) 480-8341

The Salt Lick
18300 FM 1826
Driftwood, TX 78619
(512) 858-4959

Vera's Backyard Bar-B-Qu
2404 Southmost Road
Brownsville, TX 78521
(956) 546-4159

MISSOURI
"Kansas City style"

Arthur Bryant's
1721 Brooklyn Avenue
Kansas City, MO 64127
(913) 788-7500

Fiorella's Jack Stack Barbecue
13411 Holmes Road
Martin City, MO 64145
(816) 942-9141

Gates Bar-B-Q
1325 East Emanuel Cleaver
  Boulevard
Kansas City, MO 64110
(816) 531-7522

K C Masterpiece Barbecue
4747 Wyandotte Street
Kansas City, MO 64112
(816) 531-3332

L C's Bar-B-Q
5800 Blue Parkway
Kansas City, MO 64129
(816) 417-7427

Lil' Jake's Eat It & Beat It
1227 Grand Boulevard
Kansas City, MO 64106
(816) 283-0880

Smokestack Bar-B-Q
8920 Wornall Road
Kansas City, MO 64114
(816) 444-5542

Smokestack Bar-B-Q
8250 North Church Road
Kansas City MO 64158
Phone (816) 781-7822

Smokin Joe's Bar-B-Q
101 Southwest Boulevard
Kansas City, MO 64108
(816) 421-2282

Smokin Joes Bar-B-Q
1100 Main Street
Kansas City, MO 64105
(816) 221-8821

Zap Bar-B-Q
5550 Troost Avenue
Kansas City, MO 64110
(816) 444-1119

ALABAMA

Archibald's Bar-B-Q
1211 MLK Boulevard
Northport, AL 35476
(205) 345-6861

Car-Lot BBQ
235 Bankhead Highway
Winfield, AL 35594
(205) 487-2281

Chuck's Bar-B-Q
905 Short Avenue
Opelika, AL 36801
(334) 749-4043

Big Bob Gibson's Bar-B-Q
1715 6th Avenue SE
Decatur, AL 35601
(256) 350-6969

Boar's Butt Restaurant
Highway 78 West
Winfield, AL 35594
(205) 487-6600

Bob Sykes BarB-Q
1724 9th Avenue North
Bessemer, AL 35020
(205) 426-1400

Demetri's BBQ
1901 28th Avenue South
Birmingham, AL 35209
(205) 871-1581

Dreamland Bar-B-Que
5535 15th Avenue, East
Tuscaloosa, AL 35405
(205) 758-8135

Golden Rule Bar-B-Q
2506 Crestwood Boulevard
Irondale, AL 35210
(205) 956-2678

Leo & Susie's Famous
Green Top Bar-B-Que
7530 Highway 78
Dora, AL 35062
(205) 648-9838

Rabbit's Bar-B-Q
9760 15th Street Road,
Hueytown, AL 35023
(205) 491-8498

The Bar-B-Q Place
1502 Gault Avenue South
Fort Payne, AL 35967
(256) 845-6155

The Brick Pit
5456 Old Shell Road
Mobile, AL 36608
(251) 343-0001

The Sparerib
1226 Bankhead Highway
Winfield, AL 35594
(205) 487-4148

Top Hat Barbecue
8725 U.S. Highway 31
Blount Springs, AL 35079
(256) 352-9919

ARKANSAS

Art's Barbecue & Catering
6901 Rogers Avenue
Ft Smith, AR 72903
(501) 452-2550

Couch's BBQ
5325 East Nettleton Avenue
Jonesboro, AR 72401
(870) 932-0710

Craig Brothers' Cafe
301 Walnut (Highway 70)
DeValls Bluff, AR 72041
(870) 998-2616

Gene's Barbeque
1107 N. Main Street
Brinkley, AR 72021
(870) 734-9965

HB's BBQ
6010 Lancaster Road
Little Rock, AR 72209
(501) 565-1930

Herman's Rib House
2901 College Avenue
Fayetteville, AR 72703
(501) 442-9671

Hog Pen Bar-B-Q
800 Walnut Street
Conway, AR 72032
(501) 327-5177

Lindsey's Barbecue
203 East 14th Street
North Little Rock, AR 72114
(501) 374-5901

McClard's Bar-B-Q
505 Albert Pike Road
Hot Springs, AR 71913
(501) 624-9586

Pig Pit Bar-B-Q
I-30 & Highway 7
Arkadelphia, AR 71923
(870) 246-6552

Purity Barbecue
1000 Malvern Avenue
Hot Springs, AR 71901
(501) 623-4006

Rockhouse BBQ
416 South Pine Street
Harrison, AR 72601
(501) 741-1787

Sassy Jones BBQ
105 Highway 82 East # B
Montrose, AR 71658
(870) 737-2271

Shack Bar-B-Q
608 Highway 365 North
North Little Rock, AR 72113
(501) 998-2616

Willie Mae's Rib Haus
321 West Broadway
West Memphis, AR 72303
(870) 732-0048

CALIFORNIA

Benny's Bar-B-Q
4077 Lincoln Boulevard
Marina del Rey, CA 90292
(310) 821-6939

Big Nate's
1665 Folsom Street
San Francisco, CA 94103
(415) 861-4242

Dr. Hogly Wogly's
Tyler, Texas Barbecue
8136 N. Sepulveda Boulevard
Van Nuys, CA 91402
(818) 780-6701

Everett & Jones Barbeque
2676 Fruitvale Avenue
Oakland, CA 94601
(510) 533-0900

Henry's World Famous Hi-Life
301 West Saint John Street
San Jose, CA 95110
(408) 295-5414

Memphis Minnie's
576 Haight Street
San Francisco, CA 94717
(415) 864-7675

Mr. Cecil's California Ribs
12244 West Pico Boulevard
Los Angeles, CA 90064
(310) 442-1550

Santa Maria BBQ
9552 Washington Boulevard
Culver City, CA 90232

The Bear Pit
10825 Sepulveda Boulevard
(Chatsworth Street)
Mission Hills, CA 91345
(818) 365-2500

The Pit Bar-B-Que
5309 South Vermont Avenue
Los Angeles, CA 90037
(323) 759-9428

Woody's Bar-B-Que
3446 W Slauson Avenue
Los Angeles, CA 90043
(323) 294-9443

Zeke's Smokehouse
2209 Honolulu Avenue
Montrose, CA 91020
(818) 957-7045

COLORADO

Brother Mel's BBQ
151 South College Avenue
Fort Collins, CO 80524
(970) 419-0227
Daddy Bruce's Bar-B-Que
2000 Arapahoe Avenue
Boulder, CO 80302
(303) 449-8890

KT's BBQ
7464 Arapahoe Road
Boulder, CO 80303
(303) 786-7608

Wolfe's Barbeque
333 East Colfax Avenue
Denver, CO 80203
(303) 831-1500

CONNECTICUT

Big Bubba's BBQ
1 Mohegan Sun Boulevard
Uncasville, CT 06382
(860) 862-9800

Bobby Q's Barbeque and Grill
42 Main Street
Westport, CT 06880
(203) 454-7800

Smokin' With Chris
59 West Center Street
Southington, CT 06489
(860) 620-9133

SouthernQue
70 Pomeroy Avenue
Meriden, CT 06450
(203) 238-1542

Uncle Willie's BBQ
558 Chase Avenue
Waterbury, CT 06704
(203) 596-7677

FLORIDA

Betty's Soul Food & Barbecue
601 NW 22nd Road
Fort Lauderdale, FL 33311
(954) 583-9121

Big Tim's BBQ
530 34th Street South
Street Petersburg, FL 33709
(727) 327-7388

Bubbalou's Bodacious Barbecue
5818 Conroy Road
Orlando, FL 32835
(407) 295-1212

Jazzy's BBQ
5703 West Waters Avenue
Tampa, FL 33634
(813) 243-8872

Lucille's Bad to the Bone BBQ
3011 Yamato Road
Boca Raton, FL 33434
(561) 997-9557

Shorty's BBQ Ranch
9200 S. Dixie Highway
Miami, FL 33156
(305) 670-7732

The Georgia Pig
1285 SW 40th Avenue
Fort Lauderdale, FL 33317
(954) 587-4420

Tom's Place for Ribs
1225 Palm Beach Lakes Boulevard
West Palm Beach, FL 33401
(561) 832-8774

Tom's Place
7251 North Federal Highway
Boca Raton, FL 33487
(407) 997-0920

71

GEORGIA

Ace Barbecue Barn
30 Bell Street NE
Atlanta, GA 30303
(404) 659-6630

Aleck's Barbecue Heaven
783 Martin Luther King Jr.
 Drive SW
Atlanta, GA 30314
(404) 525-2062

Country's Barbecue
1329 Broadway
Columbus, GA 31901
(706) 596-8910

Fresh Air Barbecue Place
1164 Highway 42
Flovilla, GA 30216
(770) 775-3182

Harold's Barbecue
171 Mcdonough Boulevard SE
Atlanta, GA 30315
(404) 627-9268

Jomax Bar-B-Q
1120 South Lewis Street
Metter, GA 30439
(912) 685-3636

Kelly's BBQ
2451 Highway 81
Covington, GA 30016
(770) 786-0585

Melear's
Georgia 85 (NOT the interstate)
Fayetteville, GA 30214
(770) 461-7180

Piggie Park
U.S. Highway 19 North
Thomaston, GA 30286
(706) 648-3330

Southern Pit
2964 North Expressway
Griffin, GA 30223
(770) 229-5887

The Georgia Pig
2712 U.S. Highway 17 South
Brunswick, GA 31523
(912) 264-6664

ILLINOIS

Canyon Creek Bar-B-Que
572 Randall Road
South Elgin, IL 60177
(847) 289-2121

Hickory River Smokehouse
5101 West Holiday Drive
Peoria, IL 61615
(309) 683-1227

King Barbacoa
1159 North Poplar Street
Centralia, IL 62801
(618) 545-1523

Lem's Bar-B-Q House
311 East 75th Street
Chicago, IL 60619
(773) 994-2428

Leon's Bar-B-Que
1158 West 59th Street
Chicago, IL 60619
(773) 778-7828

Russell's Barbecue
1621 North Thatcher Avenue
Elmwood Park, IL 60707
(708) 453-7065

Shemwell's Barbecue
1102 Washington Avenue
Cairo, IL 62914
(618) 734-0165

Tailgators BBQ Restaurant
6726 North Northwest Highway
Chicago, IL 60686
(773) 775-8190

INDIANA

Big Shoe's Barbecue
1105 South 12th Street
Terre Haute, IN 47802
(812) 234-0507

King Ribs Bar-B-Q
7336 Pendleton Pike
Indianapolis, IN 46226
(317) 547-5464

Pa & Ma's Barbecue Place
974 West 27th Street
Indianapolis, IN 46208
(317) 924-3698

Shyler's Bar-B-Q
405 South Green River Road
Evansville, IN 47715
(812) 476-4599

South Street Smokehouse
3305 South Street
Lafayette, IN 47904
(765) 446-0559

Wolf's Bar-B-Q Restaurant
6600 North 1st Avenue
Evansville, IN 47710
(812) 424-8891

KANSAS

Boss Hawg's Barbeque Co
2833 SW 29th Street
Topeka, KS 66614
(785) 273-7300

Famous Dave's
910 Commons Place
Manhattan, KS 66503
(785) 537-2401

Guy & Mae's Tavern
119 West William Street
Williamsburg, KS 66095
(785) 746-8830

Hayward's Pit Bar-B-Que
11051 Antioch Road
Overland Park, Kansas 66210
(913) 451-8080

Hog Wild Pit Bar-B-Q
2401 North Main Street
Hutchinson, KS 67502
(620) 669-8787

Oklahoma Joe's BBQ & Catering
3002 West 47th Avenue
Kansas City, KS 66103
(913) 722-3366

Rosedale Bar-B-Q
600 Southwest Boulevard
at Interstate 35
Kansas City, Kansas 66103
(913) 262-0343

The Pizza Parlor
1919 NE Seward Avenue,
Topeka, KS 66616
(785) 232-5190

Two Brothers BBQ
8406 West Central
Wichita, KS 67212
(316) 729-7755

Zarda BBQ & Catering
87th & Quivira
Lenexa, KS 66219
(913) 871-6798

KENTUCKY

Billy's Hickory-pit Bar-b-q
101 Cochran Road
Lexington, KY 40502
(859) 269-9593

Brother's Bar-B-Que
Covenant Shopping Center
1055 North Main Street
Madisonville, KY 42431
(270) 821-1222

Corky's Ribs & BBQ
130 West Tiverton Way
Lexington, KY 40503
(859) 272-7675
Fat Boy's Bar-B-Que
2460 Said Road
Symsonia, KY 42082
(270) 851-7744

Fat Boy's Smoking Pig
1106 Cuba Road
Mayfield, KY 42066
(270) 251-0020

George's BBQ
1362 East 4th Street
Owensboro, KY 42301
(270) 926-9276

Knoth's BBQ
728 U.S. Highway 62
Grand Rivers, KY 42045
(270) 362-8580

Moonlite Bar-B-Q
2840 West Parrish Avenue
Owensboro, KY 42301
(270) 684-8143

Old Hickory Pit Bar-B-Q
338 Washington Avenue
Owensboro, KY 42301
(270) 926-9000

Peak Brothers Drive-Inn
1800 Main Street
Waverly, KY 42462
(270) 389-0267

Pit Stop Bar-B-Que
612 South 5th Street
Louisville, KY 40202
(502) 584-4054

Roy's Bar-B-Que
Highway 68 East
Russellville, KY 42276
(270) 726-8476

Smokey Pig Bar-B-Q
2520 Louisville Road
Bowling Green, KY 42101
(270) 781-1712

Starnes BBQ
1008 Joe Clifton Drive
Paducah, KY 42001
(270) 444-9555

The Kettle Barbecue
2530 West 3rd Street
Owensboro, KY 42301
(270) 684-3800

Thomason Barbecue
701 Atkinson Street
Henderson, KY 42420
(270) 826-0654

White Light Barbecue
411 West 4th Street
Frankfort, KY 40601
(502) 223-0990

LOUISIANA

Corky's Bar-B-Q
4243 Veterans Memorial Boulevard
Metairie, LA 70006
(504) 887-5000

Country Cuisine
709 University Avenue,
Lafayette, LA 70506
(337) 269-1653

Henderson Bar-B-Que Lodge
2601 SE Evangeline Thruway
Lafayette, LA 70508
(337) 264-1373

Jay's Bar-B-Q
4215 Government Street
Baton Rouge, LA 70806
(225) 343-5082

Jim's BBQ
73658 Highway 25
Covington, LA 70471
985-809-0051

Pig Stand Restaurant
318 East Main Street
Ville Platte, LA 70586
(337) 363-2883

Poche's Market,
Restaurant, & Smokehouse
3015-A Main Highway
Breaux Bridge, LA 70517
(337) 332-2108

Ugly Dog Saloon & BBQ
401 Andrew Higgins Boulevard
New Orleans, LA 70130
(504) 569-8459

MAINE

Buck's Naked BBQ
132 U.S. Route 1
Freeport, ME 04032
(207) 865-0600

Spring Creek Bar-B-Q
26 Greenville Road
Monson, ME 04464
(207) 997-7025

Uncle Billy's BBQ
653 Congress Street
Portland, ME 04101
(207) 761-5930

MARYLAND

Andy Nelson's Barbecue
11007 York Road
Cockeysville, MD 21030
(410) 527-1226

Bear Creek Open Pit Bar-B-Q
21030 Point Lookout Road
Callaway, MD 20620
(301) 994-1030

Chubby's Southern Style Barbeque
Route 15 North at
Old Frederick Road
Emmitsburg, MD 21727
(301) 447-3322

Johnny Boy's Ribs
7530 Crain Highway
La Plata, MD 20646
(301) 392-3086

Lefty's Barbecue Unlimited, Inc.
2064 Crain Highway
Waldorf, MD 20601
(301) 638-3813

Levi's Barbeque
10252 Lake Arbor Way
Bowie, MD 20721
(301) 336-5000

O'Brien's Pit Barbecue
387 East Gude Drive
Rockville, MD 20852
(301) 340-8596

Pig Pickers Bar-B-Que
5230 Baltimore National Pike
Baltimore, MD 21229
(410) 747-5858

Piggy Wiggy's Barbecue
10092 Southern MD Boulevard
Dunkirk, MD 20754
(410) 257-4477

Randy's Ribs
Leonardtown Road
Hughesville, MD 20637
(301) 274-3525

Ribs On the Run
11410 Cherry Hill Road # 301
Beltsville, MD 20705
(301) 937-9460

Smokey's N Uncle Dave's
7300 Roosevelt Boulevard
Elkridge, MD 21075
(410) 796-0024

MASSACHUSETTS

Blue Ribbon BBQ
1375 Washington Street
West Newton, MA 01776
(617) 332 2583

BT's Smokehouse
at Village Green Campground
228 Sturbridge Road
Brimfield, MA 01010
(617) 251-6398

Bub's Barbq
676 Amherst Road
Sunderland, MA 01375
(413) 548-9630

Chili Head BBQ Co
320 West Center Street
West Bridgewater, MA 02379
(508) 941-0707

Chris Texas Bbq
1370 Dorchester Avenue
Dorchester, MA 02122
(617) 436-4700

Lester's Roadside BBQ
376A Cambridge Street (Route 3A)
Burlington, MA 01803
(781) 221-7427

Memphis Roadhouse
383 Washington Street (Route 1)
South Attleboro, MA 02703
(508) 761-5700

Uncle Pete's Hickory Ribs
72 Squire Road
Revere, MA 02151
(781) 289-7427

MINNESOTA

Baker's Ribs
8019 Glen Lane
Eden Prairie, MN 55344
(952) 942-5337

Lee & Dee's Barbeque Express
161 Victoria Street North
St. Paul, MN 55104
(651) 225-9454

Market Bar-B-Que
1414 Nicollet Avenue
Minneapolis, MN 55403
(612) 872-1111

Pastor Hamilton's Barbecue
1150 7th Street East
St. Paul, MN 55106
(651) 772-0279

Rooster's
979 Randolph Avenue
St. Paul, MN 55102
(651) 2222-0969

Scott Ja-Mama's
3 West Diamond Lake Road
Minneapolis, MN 55419
(612) 823-4450

Ted Cook's
2814 East 38th Street
Minneapolis, MN 55406
(612) 721-2023

MISSISSIPPI

Abe's Bar-B-Q Drive-In
616 State Street (Highway 61)
Clarksdale, MS 38614
(662) 624-9947

An-Jac's Famous BBQ
34 29th Street
Gulfport, MS 39507
(228) 863-5762)

E & L Barbeque
1111 Bailey Avenue
Jackson, MS 39203
(601) 355-5035

Fountain Grill
303 Highway 145 North
Aberdeen, MS 39730
(662) 369-2361

Goldie's Trail Bar-B-Que
2430 South Frontage Road
Vicksburg, MS 39180
(601) 636-9839

Hamil's Barbeque
751 Highway 51
Madison, MS 39110
(601) 856-4407

Hickory Pit
1491 Canton Mart Road
Jackson, MS 39211
(601) 956-7079

Jean's Red Door BBQ
3513 Meehan-Savoy Road South
Enterprise, MS 39330
(601) 655-8249

Leatha's BarB-Que Inn
6374 U.S. Highway 98 West
Hattiesburg, MS 39402
(601) 271-6003

Petty's BBQ
103 Highway 12 West
Starkville MS 39759
(662) 324-2363

Pig Out Inn
116S Canal Street
Natchez, MS 39120
(601) 442-8050

Spooney's Bar-Be-Que
112 East Johnson
Greenwood, MS 38930
(662) 451-7453

The Little Dooey
100 Fellowship Street
Starkville, MS 39759
(662) 323-6094

71

The Little Dooey Barbecue & Blues
701 Highway 45 North
Columbus, MS 39701
(662) 327-0088

Three Pigs BBQ
558 Southgate Road
Hattiesburg, MS 39401
(601) 545-9756

MISSOURI

Austin's Famous Bar-B-Que
6300 West Florissant Avenue
St Louis, MO 63136
(314) 382-0709

Big R's Bar-B-Q
1220 East 15th Street
Joplin, MO 64804
(417) 781-5959

Bill Sharp's Country Bar-B-Q
579 NE 50 Highway
Warrensburg, MO 65336
(660) 747-9011

Bobby Tom's Bar-B-Que
1620 Highway Z
Pevely, MO 63070
(636) 475-3400

Bo's Bar B Q Of East Prairie
111 South Lincoln Street
East Prairie, MO 63845
(573) 649-9982

Dave's Bar-B-Que
1865 Broadway Street
Cape Girardeau, MO 63701
(573) 339-1144

Dexter Bar-B-Que
1411 West Business
   U.S. Highway 60
Dexter, MO 63841
(573) 624-8810

Dexter Bar-B-Que
124 North Main
Sikeston, MO 63801
(573) 471-6676

Gary's Barbecue
56 East State Highway 162
Portageville, MO 63873
(573) 379-2333

Gates & Sons Bar-B-Q
10440 East U.S. Highway 40
Independence, MO 64055
(816) 353-5880

Greenwood Barbecue
205 East Main Street
Greenwood, MO 64034
(816) 537-5311

Homer's Bar-B-Que
693 Fisher Drive
Sullivan, MO 63080
(573) 468-4393

Hudson's Open Pit Bar-B-Que
2170 Chambers Road
St Louis, MO 63136
(314) 867-0704

Laura's & Emmie's Bar-B-Q 'N Stuff
7445 Prospect
Kansas City, MO 64132
816-361-1890

Lisa's Texas BBQ & Catering
125 Long Road
Chesterfield, MO 63005
(636) 537-0341

Lumpy's BBQ
1316 Broadway Street
Joplin, MO 64836
(417) 623-7183

Phil's Bar-B-Q
9205 Gravois Road
St Louis, MO 63123
(314) 631-7725

Pilot House
3532 Perryville Road
Cape Girardeau, MO 63701
(573) 334-7106

Raspberry's BBQ
2013 North Missouri Street #G
Macon, MO 63552
(660) 385-1436

Ribs'n Stuff
240 NW Oldham Parkway
Lees Summit, MO 64081
(816) 525-7427

Smokehouse BBQ
19000 East 39th Street South
Independence, MO 64057
(816) 795-5555

Smokin Steer BBQ & Steak House
500 South Commercial Street
Harrisonville, MO 64701
(816) 380-7800

Southern Nook Barbeque
416 East Mill Street
Liberty, MO 64068
(816) 407-1408

Three Pigs Bar-B-Q & Grill
26657 Highway 5
Gravois Mills, MO 65037
(573) 372-1800

Warehouse Bar-B-Q
and Catfish Company
729 Sunset Drive
Farmington, MO 63640
(573) 760-1600

Wicker's Bar-B-Q
501 Main Street
Hornersville, MO 63855
(573) 737-2416

NEW HAMPSHIRE

City Flame Smokehouse
363 Chestnut Street
Manchester, NH 03101
(603) 622-6022

Goody Cole's Smokehouse
374 Route 125
Brentwood, NH 03833
(603) 679-8898

KC's Rib Shack
837 Second Street
Manchester, NH 03102
(603) 627-7427

Premier Palette
946 Elm Street
Manchester, NH 03101
(603) 622-8494

NEW JERSEY

Big Ed's BBQ
305 Route 34
Old Bridge, NJ 08857
(732) 583-2626

CT's Bar-B-Que
920 Hamilton Street
Somerset, NJ 08873
(732) 418-8889

Front Street Smokehouse
1 South Front Street
Elizabeth, NJ 07202
(908) 354-1818

NEW YORK–MANHATTAN

Blue Smoke
116 East 27th Street
New York, NY 10016
(212) 447-7733

Daisy May's BBQ USA
623 11th Avenue
New York, NY 10036
(212) 977-1500

Dinosaur Bar-B-Que
646 West 131st Street
New York, NY 10027
(212) 694-1777

Hill Country Barbecue
30 West 26th Street
New York, NY 10010
(212) 255-4544

RUB (Righteous Urban Barbecue)
208 West 23rd Street
New York, NY 10011
(212) 524-4300

NEW YORK

Bailey's Smokehouse
136 Erie Street East
Blauvelt, NY 10913
(845) 398-1454

Barnstormer BBQ
50 Route 17K # K110
(Target Plaza)
Newburgh, NY 12550
(845) 568-5700

Big W's's Bar-B-Q
1475 Route 22
Wingdale, NY 12594
(845) 832-6200

Q Barbeque
112 North Main Street
Port Chester, NY 10573
(914) 933-RIBS (7427)

Southbound BBQ
301 Columbus Avenue
Valhalla, NY 10595
(914) 644-RIBS (7427)

Smokin' Al's Famous BBQ Joint
19 West Main Street
Bay Shore, NY 11706
(631) 206-3000

Tennessee Jack's BBQ
148 Carleton Avenue
East Islip, NY 11730
(631) 581-9657

Willie B's Award Winning BBQ
222 Fifth Avenue
Bay Shore, NY 11706
(631) 206-2580

OHIO

Ann's Bar-B-Que
1008 North Hawley Street
Toledo, OH 43607
(419) 241-6812

City Barbeque Inc
2111 Henderson Road
Columbus, OH 43220
(614) 336-0307

City Barbeque
5979 East Main Street
Reynoldsburg, OH 43213
(614) 583-0999

City Barbeque
4900 Reed Road, Ste. 207
Columbus, OH 43220
(614) 588-0999

Edwards Barbeque
1812 Crest Hill Avenue
Cincinnati, OH 45237
(513) 490-7029

Farris BBQ
14401 Harvard Avenue
Cleveland, OH 44128
(216) 991-3300

Flamin Pit BBQ Restaurant
1715 West Sylvania Avenue
Toledo, OH 43613
(419) 471-1410

Freddie's Southern Style Rib House
1431 Street Clair Avenue
Cleveland, OH 44114
(216) 575-1750

Golddust B B Q Co
4230 Vira Road
Stow, OH 44224
(330) 688-0722

Hot Sauce Williams
7815 Carnegie Avenue, 44103
12310 Superior Avenue, 44106
3770 Lee Road, 44128
Cleveland, OH
(216) 391-2230

Old Hickory Bar-B-Q Carryout
241 Woodman Drive
Dayton, OH 45431
(937) 253-4065

Rachel BBQ & Soul
1931 Seymour Avenue
Cincinnati, OH 45237
(513) 731-6673

R Ribs Barbeque
26004 Euclid Avenue
Cleveland, OH 44132
(216) 797-0200

71

Red Walters BBQ
8425 Cedar Avenue
Cleveland, OH 44103
(216) 791-1420

Rib Cage
1523 Baycrest Drive NW
Canton, OH 44708
(330) 452-6989

Roscoe's Ribs
415 Hillcrest Avenue
Cincinnati, OH 45125
(513) 278-5870

Shorty's Bar-B-Que
5111 Monroe Street
Toledo, OH 43623
(419) 841-9505

Smacker's Barbecue
1265 Woodville Pike
Milford, OH 45150
(513) 722-9600

Webb's Alabama Barbecue
3815 East 93rd Street
Cleveland, OH 44105
(216) 271-7039

Whitmore's
22295 Euclid Avenue, 44117
13187 Cedar Road, 44118
20209 Harvard Avenue, 44122
26006 Broadway Avenue, 44146
Cleveland, OH
(216) 579-0910

Woody & Jo's House of Ribs
222 East 5th Avenue
Columbus, OH 43201
(614) 291-0500

OKLAHOMA

Ables Western Bar-B-Que
600 East Main Street
Antlers, OK 74523
(580) 298-2573

Ables Western Bar-B-Que
800 West Main Street
Antlers, OK 74523
(580) 298-2573

Al's Barbeque
1306 South 32nd Street
Muskogee, OK 74401
(918) 683-0910

Al's Hideaway Bar-B-Q
44 SW 44th Street
OK City, OK 73109
(405) 632-1154

Banta's Ribs & Stuff
1120 North Meridian Avenue
Oklahoma City, OK 73107
(405) 946-3023

Bar B Que Express
55 Tiffany Plaza
Ardmore, Oklahoma 73401
(580) 223-8900

Charlie's Smoke House
5717 North Council Avenue
Blanchard, OK 73010
(405) 392-3990

Cookson Smokehouse Restaurant
32087 Highway 82
Cookson, OK 74427
(918) 457-4134

Country Barbeque
1934 South Cherokee Street
Muskogee, OK 74403
(918) 682-3063

Cowboy's Bar-B-Q & Grill
401 North York Street
Muskogee, OK 74403
(918) 682-0651

Crockett's Smokehouse
6901 5 May Avenue
Oklahoma City, OK 73159
(405) 681-2324

Cookson Smokehouse Restaurant
Elmer's Barbeque LLC
4130 South Peoria Avenue
Tulsa, OK 74105
(918) 742-6702

Et's Bar-B-Q & Catering
920 NE 8th Street
Oklahoma City, OK 73104
(405) 232-5150

Gary's Barbeque
3212 SE 44th Street
Oklahoma City, OK 73135
(405) 672-8818

Gary Dale's Bar-B-Q
9010 SE 29th Street
Midwest City, OK 73130
(405) 869-9434

Goodner's Smokehouse
1520 West Elk
Duncan, OK 73533
(580) 255-6181

Harv's BBQ
1332 East Lindsey Street
Norman, OK 73071
(405) 321-4492

Hick'Ry House B-B-Q
2200 South Commerce Street
Ardmore, OK 73401
(580) 223-5855

Hickr'y House
Highway 32
Marietta, OK 73448
(580) 276-3269

Jack's Bar-B-Que
4418 NW 39th Street
Oklahoma City, OK 73112
(405) 946-1865

Jim's Bar-B-Q
210 East Aeronca Drive
Midwest City, OK 73110
(405) 736-6977

John & Cook's Bar-B-Que
1310 SW 21st Street
Lawton, OK 73501
(580) 248-0036

Knotty Pine Barbeque
3301 West 5th Street
Tulsa, OK 74127
(918) 584-7354

La Fortuna Barbecue
102 North Highway 81
Duncan, OK 73533-2625
(580) 252-4245

Leo's Bar-B-Q Factory
7 Harrison Avenue
Oklahoma City, OK 73104
(405) 236-5367

Log Cabin Bar-B-Que
2840 South York Street
Muskogee, OK 74403
(918) 687-6252

Mac's Barbecue
6193 East 61st Street
Tulsa, OK 74136
(918) 481-1227

Mojo's Blues & Barbeque
509 South Cherokee Street
Catoosa, OK 74015
(918) 266-6500

Mr Sprigg's Real Pit Bar-B-Q
1017 South Air Depot Boulevard
Midwest City, OK 73110
(405) 733-8578

Mr Tee's Bar BQ
9701 NE 23rd Street
Oklahoma City, OK 73141
(405) 769-4511

My Place Bar-B-Que
4322 West Okmulgee Street
Muskogee, OK 74401
(918) 683-5202

Pete's Barbeque
3528 North Lansing Avenue
Tulsa, OK 74106
(918) 425-3373

Phipps' Bar-B-Que
116 West Main
Duncan, OK 73533
(580) 255-2020

Pig's Eye Inc.
2006 North Broadway Avenue
Ada, OK 74820
(580) 310-6039

Porkys BBQ
2804 South Highway 81
El Reno, OK 73036
(405) 422-2911

Rib Crib Barbecue
3232 West Skelly Drive
Tulsa, OK 73099
(918) 447-1400

Rib Crib Barbecue
3022 South Garnett
Tulsa, OK 74129
(918) 828-0010

Rib Crib Barbecue
1601 South Harvard
Tulsa, OK 74112
(918) 742-2742

Rib Crib Barbecue
8040 South Yale
Tulsa, OK 74136
(918) 492-8627

Rib Crib Barbecue
5025 Sheridan Road
Tulsa, OK 74145
(918) 663-4295

Rib Crib Barbecue
1223 South Meridian Avenue
OK City, OK 73108
(405) 917-7400

Rib Crib Barbecue
401 SW 74th Street
Oklahoma City, OK 73139
(405) 616-7800

Ribs N Bibs
444 South 4th
Ketchum, OK 74349
(918) 782-1936

Roy's Backyard BBQ & Grill
183 & Iris
Hobart, OK 73651
(580) 726-3277

Roy's Bar BQ
309 West Missouri Avenue
Chickasha, OK 73018
(405) 224-9843

Smokehouse Bob's Bar-B-Que
1100 North 11th Street
Muskogee, OK 74401
(918) 687-0275

Stagecoach Bar-B-Q
400 West South Street
Newkirk, OK 74647
(580) 362-3160

Suzie Q's Barbeque
1442 County Road 1590
Marlow, OK 73055
(580) 658-6681

Tom's Barbecue
2504 NE 10th Street
Oklahoma City, OK 73117
(405) 427-3898

Tony O'z Bar-B-Que & Chili
1156 South Garnett Road
Tulsa, OK 74128
(918) 438-2410

Turkey Creek BBQ
212 East Lahoma Road
Lahoma, OK 73754
(580) 796-9200

Uncle John's Smokestack
24 East 33rd Street
Edmond, OK 73013
(405) 359-7576

Uncle Mike's Bar-B-Que
11326 Highway 59 North
Grove, OK 74344
(918) 786-3344

PENNSYLVANIA

Eddie's Bar B Que Chickens
1339 West Olney Avenue
Philadelphia, PA 19141
(215) 424-2012

Miss Amelia's Bar B Que
914 North 2nd Street
Philadelphia, PA 19123
(800) 232-2004

Mr C's Bar-Be-Que
5724 Old York Road
Philadelphia, PA 19141
(215) 224-2356

Mr C's Bar Be Que
3750 Germantown Avenue
Philadelphia, PA 19140
(215) 223-8500

Phoebe's Bar BQ
2214 South Street
Philadelphia, PA 19146
(215) 546-4811

Randall's Barbeque
122 South Water Street West
Newton, PA 15089
(724) 872-2240

Rib Ranch
2401 East Venango Street #2401
Philadelphia, PA 19134
(215) 533-7427

Ron's Rib
1627 South Street
Philadelphia, PA 19146
(215) 545-9160

Smoking Dudes BBQ Company
3400 Neshaminy Boulevard
Bensalem, PA 19020
(215) 752-5500

Tommy Gunn's American Barbecue
4901 Ridge Avenue
Philadelphia, PA 19128
(215) 508-1030

Wilson's Bar-B-Q
700 North Taylor Avenue
Pittsburgh, PA 15212
(412) 322-7427

SOUTH CAROLINA

Big D's BBQ Barn
350 George Bishop Parkway
Myrtle Beach, SC 29579
(843) 236-4666

Big E's Seafood and BBQ
Highway 9 East
Longs, SC 29568
(843) 399-3999

Big T's BBQ
2520 Congaree Road
Gadsden, SC 29568
(803) 353-0488

Brown's BBQ
439 Highway 52 North
Moncks Corner, SC 29461
(843) 761-5440

Bryan's Pink Pig
Highway 170 A
Hardeeville, SC 29927
(843) 784-3635

Countryside BBQ
470 U.S. Highway 378
West McCormick, SC 29835
(803) 637-6350

D & H BBQ
412 South Mill
Manning, SC 29102
(803) 435-2189

Dacusville Smokehouse
2801 Dacusville Highway
Easley, SC 29640
(864) 855-5431

Duke's BBQ
949 Robertson Boulevard
Walterboro, SC 29488
(843) 549-1446

Earl Duke's BBQ
789 Chestnut Street
Orangeburg, SC 29115
(803) 534-9418

Gore's Bar-B-Que Country Kitchen
818 N Main Street
Aynor, SC 29511
(843) 358-1150)

Hudson's Smokehouse
4952 Sunset Boulevard
Lexington, SC 29072
(803) 356-1070

Jackie Hite's Barbecue
Highway 23
Leesville, SC 29006
(803) 532-3354

JB's Smokeshack
3406 Maybank Highway
Johns Island, SC 29455
(843) 557-0426)

JD's Pig N Chicken
3010 Highway 17 South
Garden City Beach, SC 29576
(843) 357-0989

Jim 'n Nicks
288 King Street
Charleston, SC 29401
(843) 577-0406

Little Pig's Barbecue of Anderson
1401 North Main Street
Anderson, SC 29621
(864) 226-7388

McCabe's Bar-B-Q
480 North Brooks Street
Manning, SC 29102
(803) 435-2833

Maurice's Piggy Park
1601 Charleston Highway
Columbia, SC 29169
(803) 796-0220

Melvin's Bar B Que
538 Folly Road, 29412
925 Houston Northcutt Boulevard
Charleston, SC 29464

Po Pigs Bo-B-Q
2410 Highway 174
Edisto Island, SC 29438
(843) 869-9007

Radd Dew's BBQ
3430 Highway 701 South
Conway, SC 29527
(843) 397-3453

Richard's BBQ
3944 Main Street
Loris, SC 29569
(843) 756-3090

Shealy's BBQ House
340 East Columbia Avenue
Leesville, SC 29070
(803) 532-8135

Shuler's B-B-Que
419 Highway 38 West
Latta, SC 29565
(843) 752-4700

Sticky Fingers
235 Meeting Street
Charleston, SC 29401
(843) 853-7427

Sweatman's BBQ
Route 453 (Eutaville Road)
Holly Hill, SC 29059
(843) 563-7574

The Hickory Hawg
2770 Maybank Highway
Charleston, SC 29455
(843) 557-1121)

TENNESSEE

Bill's Bar-B-Q
531 South Church Street
Henderson, TN 38340
(731) 989-4075

Bobby's BBQ
(at Jack's Creek community)
6060 State Route 100 East
Henderson, TN 38340
(731) 989-2242

Bozo's Hot Pit Bar-B-Q
342 Highway 70 West
Mason, Tennessee 38049
(901) 294-3400

Foster's Bar-B-Q
2650 Highway 100
Reagan, TN 38368
(731) 968-1046

Hays Smoke House
16319 Highway 412 East
Lexington, TN 38351
(731) 967-3222

Hog Heaven
115 27th Avenue North
Nashville, TN 37203
(615) 329-1234

Jack's Bar-B-Que
416 Broadway
Nashville, TN 37203
(615) 254-5715

Jack's Bar-B-Que
334 West Trinity Lane
Nashville, TN 37207
(615) 228-9888

Joyner's Jacks Creek Bar-B-Que
10 State Route 22A North
Jacks Creek, TN 38347
(731) 989-4140

Judge Bean's BBQ
123 12th Avenue North
Nashville, TN 37203
(615) 244-8884

My Three Sons Bar-B-Q
311 North Church Avenue,
Henderson, TN 38340
(731) 989-9700

Nolen's Barbecue No 3
115 East James Campbell
  Boulevard
Columbia, TN 38401
(931) 381-4322

Papa KayJoe's
Bar-B-Que
119 West Ward Street
Centerville, TN 37033
(931) 729-2131

Ridgewood Barbecue
900 Elizabethton Highway
Bluff City, TN 37618
(423) 538-7543

Scott's-Parker's Bar-B-Q
10880 Highway 412 West
Lexington, TN 38351
(731) 968-0420

Shuford's Smokehouse
924 Signal Mountain Road
Chattanooga, TN 37405
(423) 267-0080

VIRGINIA

Allman's Bar-B-Que
1299 Jefferson Davis Highway
Fredericksburg, VA 22401
(540) 373-9881

BBQ Country
9719 James Madison Highway
Warrenton, VA 20186
(540) 439-6904

Bill's BBQ
5805 West Broad Street
Richmond, VA 23230
(804) 282-8539

Bubba's Best Barbeque
1134 West Main Street
Abingdon, VA 24210
(540) 676-2241

Buz and Ned's Real BBQ
1119 North Boulevard
Richmond, VA 23230
(804) 355-6055

Cowling's Bar-B-Q
7019 General Mahone Highway
Waverly, VA 23890
(804) 834-3100

Cuz's Uptown Barbeque
U.S. Route 460
Pounding Mill, VA 24637
(276) 964-9014

Dixie Bones
13440 Occoquan Road
Route 1
Woodbridge, VA 22191
(703) 492-2205

Doumar's Cones & Barbecue
1919 Monticello Avenue
Norfolk, VA 23517
(757) 627-4163

Dunn's Drive In Barbecue
3716 Mechanicsville Pike
Richmond, VA 23223
(804) 329-4676

Flavors Soul Food
3420 Carlyn Hill Drive
Falls Church, VA 22041
(703) 379-4411

Hawk's BBQ
2311 West Broad Street
Richmond, VA 23220
(804) 359-9333

King Street Blues
112 North Street Asaph Street
Alexandria, VA 22314
(703) 836-8800

King's Barbecue
2910 South Crater Road
Petersburg, VA 23805
(804) 732-0975

Olde Virginia Barbecue
35 Meadow View Avenue
Rocky Mount, VA 24151
(540) 489-1788

Pierce's Pit Barbecue
910 Atlantic Avenue
Virginia Beach, VA 23451
(757) 491-6218

Sibley's Bar-B-Q
4412 West Hundred Road
Chester, VA 23831
(804) 748-3299

Smokey Pig
212 South Washington Highway
Ashland, VA 23005
(804) 798-4590

The Mighty Midget Kitchen,
202 Harrison Street SE
Leesburg, VA 20175
(703) 777-6406

Willard's Real Pit BBQ,
4300 Chantilly Shopping Center
Chantilly, VA 20151
(703) 488-9970

WASHINGTON, D.C.

Old Glory All-American Bar-B-Que
3139 M Street NW
Washington, D.C. 20007
(202) 337-3406

The Rib Pit
3903 14th Street NW
Washington, D.C. 20011
(202) 829-9747

WISCONSIN

BBQ Time
1215 DeKoven Avenue
Racine, WI 53403
(262) 633-8585

Brew City Barbeque
125 East Juneau Avenue
Milwaukee, WI 53202
(414) 278-7033

Famous Dave's Bar-B-Que
3030 Milton Avenue
Janesville, WI 53545
(608) 757-8100

Grandma's Favorite Recipes
321 8th Street South
La Crosse, WI 54601
(608) 782-4853

Speed Queen Barbecue
1130 West Walnut Street
Milwaukee, WI 53205
(414) 265-2900

WYOMING

Bigns Smoke House
10634 Highway 189
Big Piney, WY 83113
(307) 276-5633

Blues Bar-B-Q
1062 East Brundage Lane
Sheridan, WY 82801
(307) 674-1773

Bubba's Bar-B-Que Restaurant
515 West Broadway
Jackson, WY 83001
(307) 733-2288

Elk Country Bar Bq
709 West Pine
Pinedale, WY 82941
(307) 367-2252

71

INDEX